# And Here We Are
# At The Table

**Ariana Mullins**

ISBN: 978-1500632090

ISBN-13: 1500632090

# DEDICATION

This book is dedicated to my husband Jeff,
and my daughter Amelia.
You are the people I enjoy cooking for the most,
and who make our table–
wherever in the world it may happen to be–
a wonderful place to spend time.
You make my life very sweet.

.

# Contents

# Introduction

**At the table** is where the good stuff happens. Gathering around a delicious meal with friends and family has been a source of joy and nourishment for people through the ages, and is something we all deeply need. It's a time of good conversation, connection, and revival. So many elements of our modern lives are crowding out this tradition, but I believe it's more important than ever before to spend time together at the table, and that it doesn't have to be difficult to share beautiful meals on a daily basis.

A little over four years ago, my family made the switch to a grain-free diet. This was for a number of reasons (more on that later) but I quickly learned that eating this way is really not too hard, and it's *at least* as delicious as the standard diet, if not more. Going into this change, I had the advantage of having lived and eaten great meals in many different countries. Many food cultures don't rely heavily on grains, and it was easy to see that one of the best ways to enjoy this new way of eating is to take flavors and food combinations from other regions.

I started sharing my family's favorite recipes on my blog, AndHereWeAre.net, and these meal ideas proved to be very popular. In writing this cookbook, I hope to help you bring lots of great flavors and times of warmth and connection to your table. And if you are struggling with making the switch, I have a lot of tips and resources for you in the back of this book.

Although I'm an American, I grew up in the Philippines, and have lived and traveled all over the world. The food I cook and eat is a reflection of these life experiences. In the last several years, my family has lived in Los Angeles, Portland, Germany, and England. We are also on our way to a new adventure, living in Spain, in February 2015.

## So, how does my family eat?

We try our best to eat with the seasons, and to buy food that is organic and humanely produced. Also, we generally follow a grain-free diet. This is for a number of reasons– a combination of food allergies (my husband and daughter) and an auto-immune disease (me) and some other things that bothered us for a few years. We made the switch nearly four years ago, and love our food and the way our food choices make us feel. Quality ingredients are super important, and I make almost everything we eat (from bone broths to salad dressing to mayonnaise to sauerkraut) from scratch. We don't get hung up on food substitutes– most of our meals are made up of vegetables and an animal protein source. And it's delicious!

That said, I am not interested in a bunch of eating rules, and feel sad when I see people getting stressed out about what to eat.

For me, food is all about enjoying life. Real food tastes fantastic, and it feels good inside our bodies. I don't believe in food-related guilt, and lots of rules. It's important to know what works for your body, and then to simply find pleasure in your meals, and to eat as often as you can with people you love.

# Let's Eat.

Breakfast

I have always taken my breakfasts very seriously. Maybe it's just because I love morning and I love eating-- and eating in the morning just feels amazing. Maybe it's because I love bacon and eggs and all the other breakfast foods. Frankly, it doesn't matter why. I am just glad that I get a fresh crack at it every single day.

In our home, we eat a lot of eggs, bacon and fruit. We do make grain-free muffins and pancakes on the weekends, but most of the recipes I come up with myself are related to eggs.

We had our own chickens for years, and there is something wonderful about collecting eggs from the hens in the morning, grabbing some garden greens, and making a meal from it, just minutes later. These days, we buy our free range eggs from a lady who sells them on her doorstep. She writes a little note on the boxes to let us know when we might find a green egg inside, laid by an Auracana hen named Margot. (More on that later.)

One of my favorite meals to have friends over for is brunch. There is something really nice about spending a Saturday morning together at the table, with lots of coffee, chatting and eating our fill. I have included quite a few recipes that are perfect for this occasion.

# The Almond Dutch Baby

Sometimes we want protein for breakfast, but need a break from all of the savory preparations and the monotony of scrambled eggs. The Almond Dutch Baby is just right. I invented this little breakfast dish when I had a baby, and wanted something comforting but sufficiently hearty in the morning, with little effort. This recipe is very forgiving, and can take on many variations, based on what you have on hand. The Almond Dutch Baby will become one of those things that you don't need a recipe for after making it a few times, as you will soon learn that you can change it up in a hundred different ways without fear of failure. This recipe serves 1, but it's easy to double or triple!

Note: I have made larger batches of this, and simply cooked it in a buttered pie pan in the oven, and sliced it into wedges. That worked out beautifully, too.

I hope that this recipe will bring a little extra comfort and happiness to your mornings, and sustaining power to keep you going strong as you go about your day.

Ingredients

1 teaspoon butter or coconut oil

3 pastured eggs

2 tablespoons cream, plain yogurt or coconut milk

2 tablespoons almond flour

2 tablespoons unsweetened shredded coconut

1 teaspoon sweetener, such as honey or maple syrup

a dash of cinnamon

1/4 teaspoon almond or vanilla extract

a tiny pinch of sea salt

as for equipment, you will want a small oven-proof skillet

Instructions

Preheat oven to 400° F (200° C.)

In a small oven-proof skillet over low heat, melt the butter or coconut oil.

Combine the eggs and all of the rest of the ingredients in a bowl, and whisk together until combined.

When your butter/ oil is bubbling a bit in the pan, pour in the batter. Cook over medium heat for 1-2 minutes, to cook the bottom portion of the breakfast cake.

Transfer the skillet to the oven, and bake until the top is golden and puffed up. Don't expect it to puff as dramatically as a traditional Dutch Baby, because the almond flour and high volume of eggs will make it more dense. The main thing to look for is the golden top.

Release the Dutch baby onto a plate (using a spatula) and serve with butter and jam or apple sauce.

# The Caramelized Apple Dutch Baby

I have to tell you about this variation of the Grain-Free Almond Dutch Baby. It's my favorite fall breakfast, made with gingery, caramelized apples. This breakfast feels fancy, but it's pretty easy– *so* worth taking the time to caramelize some apples. This recipe serves 1, but it's easy to double or triple!

You can also make larger batches of this, to serve more than one– simply cook the apples and put them in a buttered pie pan in the oven, pour the batter over, and put it in the hot oven. Slice it into wedges to serve. We like it this way on the weekends, when we're all enjoying it together.

## Ingredients

1 tablespoon butter, ghee or coconut oil
(If you're using butter, add a little coconut oil or even a few drops of olive oil to keep it from browning.)

1/2 an apple, cut into three wedges, then chopped cross-wise to make thin triangles

2 teaspoons sweetener, such as maple syrup or brown sugar

a dash of cinnamon

1/2 teaspoon freshly grated or finely chopped ginger root

3 pastured eggs

2 tablespoons cream, plain yogurt, or coconut milk

2 tablespoons almond flour

2 tablespoons unsweetened, shredded coconut
1/4 teaspoon vanilla extract

a tiny pinch of sea salt

as for equipment, you will want a small (5-6 inch) oven-proof skillet

## Instructions

Preheat oven to 400° F (200° C.)

In a small oven-proof skillet over low heat, melt the butter or coconut oil.

Add the apple slices, and sauté for about two minutes, until they begin to soften. Add 1 teaspoon of brown sugar (or other sweetener) and the cinnamon and ginger. Continue to sauté for about five more minutes, until the apples are beginning to brown a bit and get sticky. While they are cooking you can mix the other ingredients together.

Combine the eggs and all of the rest of the ingredients in a bowl, and whisk together until combined.

Pour your batter over the apples.

Cook over medium heat for 1-2 minutes, to cook the bottom portion of the breakfast cake. Transfer the skillet to the oven, and bake until the top is golden and puffed up. Don't expect it to puff as dramatically as a traditional Dutch Baby, because the almond flour and high volume of eggs will make it more dense. The main thing to look for is the golden top.

Invert the pan and release the Dutch baby onto a plate (using a spatula) and serve with butter and maple syrup, if desired.

# Shakshukah

Have you heard of Shakshukah before? A couple of years ago, when I was feeling kind of desperate for some stimulating food, we took a trip to London just for three days of non-stop eating. One of the highlights was a Mediterranean breakfast at a cafe called Fernandez & Wells. My daughter Amelia had morcilla sausage and two fried eggs, while Jeff and I each had a small skillet of eggs poached in and incredible tomato sauce with peppers and spices. I don't think they called it Shakshukah on the menu, because I'm pretty sure I would have made a note of it. This is a popular dish in Northern Africa, and there are many different versions of it out there– also spelled chakchouka or shakshuka, even tsakstouka. It wasn't until I saw a post from David Lebovitz, based on a recipe in the cookbook Jerusalem, that I was sure what the name of the dish was that I'd been craving. As soon as I saw the pictures, I had intense hunger pangs.

I went to bed thinking about it, and woke up the next morning with firm resolve to make it. Rather than waiting till a more reasonable time, I made my family get dressed and walk to the supermarket with me, so I could buy the ingredients to make it for breakfast. Everyone decided it was well worth the effort. Traditionally, this dish is served with lots of crusty bread to mop up the tomato sauce with. We improvised with broiled eggplant slices, which did the job very nicely. I like to double the batch of sauce, and save it to make a quick batch, or a really wonderful frittata. It also works great as a sauce for veggies. Serves 2-3

## Ingredients

2 tablespoons olive oil, ghee, or bacon drippings

1 medium onion, peeled and diced

3 cloves garlic, peeled and chopped

1/2 – 1 chile pepper, stemmed, sliced in half and deseeded, finely diced/minced or some chile flakes, to taste (optional)

1 1/2 teaspoons salt

1 teaspoon freshly ground black pepper

1 teaspoon smoked paprika

1 teaspoon caraway seeds, crushed

1 teaspoon cumin seeds crushed, or 3/4 teaspoon ground cumin

1/2 teaspoon turmeric

two 14-ounce cans of diced or crushed tomatoes

2 tablespoons tomato paste

2 teaspoons honey

1 teaspoon red wine vinegar

1 cup (20g) loosely packed, roughly chopped greens– I like tatsoi, and sometimes substitute summer squash for the greens

4 ounces (about 1 cup, 115g) feta cheese, cut in generous, bite-sized cubes (optional)

4 to 6 eggs

a small bunch chopped fresh parsley (cilantro would also be good)

## Instructions

Heat the oil in a large skillet or a pot, and add the diced onion. Sauté for three minutes or so, add the garlic, and cook for another minute.

Add all of the spices to the onion mixture, and cook until very fragrant, about two minutes.

Add the tomatoes, tomato paste, honey, and cider vinegar, as well as the salt. Let it cook down for about 15 minutes, adding the greens halfway through. Use a spatula to scrape the sides and bottom of the pan now and then.

Once the sauce has thickened, taste for saltiness and acidity, and adjust the seasonings.

Now, you have a couple options– you could cook all of the eggs together in the skillet, or you could make up individual servings. I usually choose the latter.

Spoon the tomato sauce into individual skillets or oven-safe dishes. Press chunks of feta into the sauce at regular intervals, and then make little wells to accommodate the eggs. Crack your eggs into the tomato sauce, and run a spoon through the whites to let them mingle with the sauce (but don't break the yolks!)

You can bake these off in an oven, or cook them on the stovetop. Gently simmer them on the stovetop for about 10 minutes, checking that the whites get cooked through, but the yolks stay soft. I find that covering them helps. Or, you can bake them in the oven at 375° (175° C) for 10-15 minutes. Again, you are watching the yolks, so they don't overcook.

Garnish with plenty of fresh parsley.

# A Very Charming Way to Buy Eggs...

**How do you buy your eggs?** The luckiest ones among you have chickens, and just take a stroll into your back yard to pick up your breakfast ingredients. While that worked for us for a while, we ended up re-homing our chickens recently. I was sad to give up that part of my self-sufficiency dream for now, but I have found another wonderful way to get very free-range eggs. But it does take a little (literal) legwork.

I grab some empty egg cartons, and take a walk toward town. After one busy intersection, it's all brick-lined walkways. I love this about England.

Ten minutes of enjoying the old architecture and peeking into gardens, and I am in for a lovely view.

I step into this little nook of herbs and potted shrubs, and take a moment.

Ah, yes. There's the abbey. This view always makes me smile– how rare for an American to enjoy such a view near her own home!

Then we turn right, and we're almost there.

We pass the "mini mart" on the right, but we'll come back to that in a moment. Turn left at the dark grey door. And here we are!

These are the free range eggs I'm after, at the best price in town! Sometimes they are special– you pay a little more for larger eggs or green Auracana eggs, and a little less for smaller or irregularly shaped eggs.

Once I have returned my empty cartons, collected my eggs and slipped my money through the mail slot, I backtrack a few doors to the "mini mart" on the corner.

How sweet is this little setup? Here, we buy raw honey, potatoes, apples, potted plants, and any other interesting things I might find. Recently, I bought chestnuts, walnuts, quinces and medlars grown in the neighborhood. It is all extremely local, and the proceeds are donated to raise funds for charity. I love eating greens and goodies from other people's back gardens. Not only is this community-strengthening and budget-friendly, but it's an absolute pleasure.

So, I fill up my backpack with anything I can use, slip my money through the mail slot again, and it's home again, home again, jiggety-jig. Enjoying more architecture and old-world vignettes along the way, of course.

I never buy too many eggs at a time– why would I cheat myself out of another trip?
**Thanks for coming along with me this time!**

# The Hedonist's Breakfast &
# Hollandaise Sauce for One (or 10!)

I don't know what took me so long to make Hollandaise Sauce. Maybe it was because every time I read a recipe for it, the author felt the need to describe how easily it could all go wrong. But I actually really love Hollandaise sauce, and often dream of the Eggs Benedict at one of our favorite breakfast places in Portland.

I've come to terms with the fact that I'm probably not going to find a breakfast to get very excited about in my small English town, so I am working on expanding the offerings at my own breakfast table. I took a look at a slew of recipes out there on the internet, and came up with a scheme for making any amount of Hollandaise sauce, without having to reference a recipe each time. I most frequently make it for one. *That's right.* I love making myself an elaborate breakfast, when everyone else is gone, and it's just me and my coffee, and a view of our garden.

This is kind of an anti-recipe– just some basic proportions. I've made it dozens of times, and I have yet to mess it up, even with my very loose way of measuring things. And the ingredients are so basic, you can make a phenomenal meal with very little on hand. Don't tell anyone, but we like to dip our

# Hollandaise Sauce for One

This sauce seems to be pretty easy-going. Since everything is a either a teaspoon or tablespoon or a pinch, it is extremely simple to make it with as many yolks as you'd like, so it can be just for you, or to share with the whole family.

Ingredients

1 egg yolk

1 tablespoon hot water

sea salt

1 teaspoon lemon juice (please, from a real lemon)

1 tablespoon butter (the better your butter, the better your sauce)

cayenne pepper

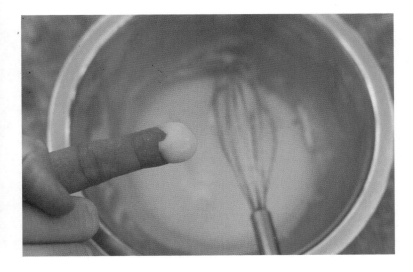

Instructions

Put the egg yolk in a small metal bowl. Whisk it a little. Add a tablespoon of hot water (I am usually simmering some water in preparation of cooking the sauce, and then poaching eggs, so this works out very conveniently) and a pinch of sea salt.

Whisk it some more, then add roughly a teaspoon of lemon juice, and a tablespoon (roughly– I have never actually measured it) of butter.

Put the metal bowl over a simmering pot of water. Whisk. The higher the heat and boil of your water, obviously, the faster it will cook– but then there's a higher need to be paying close attention and whisking constantly. I keep mine a little lower, and give myself the leisure of chopping up some greens as I whisk– but still put in the time whisking well. The butter will melt, everything will blend together, and gradually begin to thicken.

It's up to you how thick you want it to be– keep in mind that you will probably want it to be oozy versus gloppy, and it will thicken slightly more as it cools.

Taste it. Decide what it needs more of, and add the cayenne pepper, if you like. I have also added a little olive oil to balance the flavors a bit, and haven't gotten in trouble for adding that, more butter, or even lemon juice after it has thickened. For the record, I have also made this with white wine vinegar, when I didn't have much lemon on hand (some recipes use mostly white wine vinegar anyhow).

And that's it! It's really not too tricky, and always delicious.

# The Hedonist's Breakfast

Here's the breakfast I love to make with this sauce, and the order of business:

## Ingredients

2 eggs

1 recipe Hollandaise Sauce

2 cups greens, washed

1 teaspoon butter

salt to taste

## Instructions

Heat a small pot of water, and make the Hollandaise Sauce.

Whilst getting that done, crack a couple of eggs to poach in the hot water, and chop some greens. When the sauce is done, you can either blanch the greens in the hot water you'll use for the eggs, thus getting three uses out of that one pot of water, or you can cook your greens another way– a quick sauté or blanching them in a separate pot.

Poach your eggs.*

Put your greens in a dish after draining them well, and salt and butter them.

Eggs go on top. And, of course, the Hollandaise Sauce makes it all very special.

(Bacon is technically optional, but will make you much happier if you are anything like me. If you will be adding bacon, just put it on a baking sheet at 400° F (200° C) for about 15 minutes before you get started, flipping halfway through.)

* A word about poaching eggs: I know it can seem intimidating, if you haven't done it before. It took me a while to get up the courage to assemble a carton full of eggs that I planned on sacrificing for the sake of learning to do it. Don't be scared. I'll explain how on the next page, and soon you'll be poaching like a champ. Alternatively, you can just cook them over-easy in a frying pan!

# How to Poach Eggs

Ingredients for this are very simple: eggs, white wine vinegar, a deep pan, a slotted spoon, and a clean kitchen towel or paper towels.

Instructions

Fill a deep pan with about 4-5 inches of water.

Bring the water to a simmer– when there are steadily breaking bubbles on the surface. Add a splash of white wine vinegar. Using a whisk, rapidly swirl the water around to create a vortex.

Break an egg into a ramekin or cup and pour it slowly into the water, white first. When you do this, keep the lip of the ramekin close to the water so the egg goes in as gently as possible.

Allow the egg to set around the yolk. When the white is set, the egg should begin to float toward the surface of the water. Expect it to cook for
about three minutes.

Use a slotted spoon to gently ease the egg out of the water.

Gently place the egg onto paper towels or a kitchen towel (what I use) to absorb the extra water, before putting it on the dish you will be serving.

# Sunny Eggs with Spring Onions

This recipe is perfect for the beginning of spring, when there are plenty of onions to thin from the garden. You can use the bulb and the green leaves, too, which is handy. The eggs take on an unexpected, bright florescent yellow hue from the green parts of the onions, and it's pretty. (Serves 2)

Ingredients

2 tablespoons butter

2-4 spring onions depending on size– bulbs and stalks

4 pastured eggs

salt and pepper

pecorino cheese, optional

Instructions

Put a small skillet over medium to low heat, and melt the butter in it.

While the butter is melting, quickly chop the onion bulbs into rings, or in half lengthwise and into strips, if larger. Put those in the sizzling butter, and sauté for 3 minutes.

Roughly chop the green parts of the onions, and add to the skillet, moving it all around with a spatula. Season with a little salt.

Crack the eggs on top of the onions, sprinkle with a little salt, and cover the pan. (A plate will do if you don't have a lid the right size.)

Let cook over low heat until the whites are opaque, but don't overcook the yolks. It helps to turn the heat off just before they are done, and let them sit covered for a minute.

Season with freshly-ground pepper. If you have some pecorino cheese, grate a little on top.

# Greek Herb Frittata

When there is an abundance of fresh herbs in your life, thank your lucky stars, and make this dish. The flavors are so bright and cheerful, and this frittata works well for any meal of the day. If you're having it for a light dinner, pair it with a simple green salad and a glass of wine. (Serves 2-3)

Ingredients

1 tablespoon butter

1 small white onion, diced

tender greens like radish or young beet greens, or spinach (optional)

6 pastured eggs

1/4 cup Greek-style yogurt or sour cream

at least two of the following, and of course using all would be wonderful: 1/4 cup freshly chopped flat-leaf parsley, dill, basil, cilantro

2 tablespoon finely chopped fresh mint (optional)

2 tablespoons finely chopped green onions (optional)

1/3 cup crumbled tangy feta cheese

salt and pepper to taste

Instructions

Preheat an oven to 375° F (190° C.)

Melt butter over medium-low heat in a medium-sized skillet, and add the chopped onions. Sauté gently as you do the next two steps.

While the onions cook, crack the eggs into a large bowl, and whisk with the yogurt or sour cream, until they are well-mixed.

Add the fresh herbs and feta to the egg mixture, and season with salt and pepper.

Once the onions are translucent, add the greens, if using, and cook for 1 minute. Pour the egg mixture into the skillet, and give a quick stir with a spatula to mix the onions into the eggs.

Put the skillet of eggs into the oven, and bake for 20 minutes, until the top is turning golden, and the body of the frittata is puffy and no longer jiggly. You can test for done-ness by making a little slit in the center with a knife, and looking to see if it's still runny inside.

Slice into wedges and serve with fresh fruit and a green salad.

# Apple, Leek & Bacon Breakfast Sausage

We always eat protein in the morning over here, and since anything (even bacon!) can get a little boring day after day, we try to mix it up without getting too fussy about it on the weekdays. That's why making sausage patties and then freezing them is perfect. You can make as many as you want when you have the time, and enjoy them for days. I've experimented a lot with a recipe for breakfast patties, and I think I have it just right.

This recipe makes 14-18 patties, depending on the size.

## Ingredients

4-5 thick-cut strips of smoked bacon

3/4 cup chopped leeks (white ends)

1 medium apple, cored and quartered (no need to peel, if organic)

1 tablespoon fresh or dried rosemary

2 tablespoons fresh chopped sage leaves (or 2 teaspoons of dried)

1 tablespoon molasses

1/2 tablespoon fresh lemon juice or apple cider vinegar

1/2 teaspoon ground black pepper

1- 2 teaspoons sea salt depending on personal taste

1/4 teaspoon ground cloves

a dash of cayenne powder

1 kilo or 2 lbs. ground pork

## Instructions

First of all, you have an option of firming up the bacon a little, to give the sausage more body and a little less flab. You can do this by baking the strips of bacon on a baking sheet at 400° F (200° C) for a few minutes, until the rashers are about half-way done– this takes out some of the moisture, and a little bit of the grease. You can absolutely skip this step, too. I've done it both ways, and I prefer to make the sausages with slightly-cooked bacon.

Put all of the ingredients except for the pork into your food processor, and whiz until everything is pretty finely chopped. Once it's all evenly chopped up, add the ground pork, and just pulse for a couple of seconds until it looks like it's all mixed well– if you go too long, it makes the texture too crumbly.

If this is your first time making them, I would suggest getting out a pan and throwing a little bit of the mixture in to cook and taste. Then you'll know if you need a little extra salt or acid, before making them into patties.

Cook in a skillet until cooked through, or bake them in the oven at 350° F (180° C) for 20-30 minutes– a great way to prepare a lot of them for brunch!

Enjoy!

# BLT Breakfast Salad

This is a great brunch dish, or a cool breakfast for a warm morning. I like to have this one when I've had my fill of eggs, but adding quartered hard boiled eggs also works really well if you need the extra protein. Serves 2, but it's easy to increase for any number of servings.

## Ingredients

1 small head butter lettuce

3 ripe tomatoes, quartered

1/4 of an English cucumber, thinly sliced

half of a ripe avocado, sliced

4 slices cooked bacon (more if the slices are very thin) chopped into half-inch pieces

2 hard boiled eggs, quartered, optional

2 tablespoons fresh parsley, chopped

1 tablespoon fresh dill, chopped (fennel fronds are a good substitute here)

salad dressing to taste: either Karen's Spanish Vinaigrette (page 62), Creamy Lemon & Dill Dressing (page 64), or olive oil and vinegar to taste

salt and pepper to taste

## Instructions

Tear or chop the lettuce and arrange on a serving dish.

Evenly arrange the tomatoes, cucumber, and avocado on top of the lettuce.

Top with the bacon, and add the slices of hard-boiled eggs, if using.

Sprinkle the herbs on top, and dress the salad with dressing of choice, and season with salt and pepper.

# Apple & Nut Cereal

This recipe is a throwback to my vegan days. It's perfect for when you want something light and sweet, and have overdosed on bacon and eggs. My daughter loves it, too. Feel free to substitute any nuts, seeds, or dried fruit you have on hand. you have on hand. (This makes 1-2 servings.)

Ingredients

1/4 cup almonds

2 tablespoons raisins

1 apple, cored and chopped

1/4 teaspoon cinnamon

2 tablespoons unsweetened shredded coconut

a milk option– this can be actual cow's milk, cream, almond milk, fresh coconut milk (made by blending coconut with hot water and straining) or banana milk (add 1/2 a banana to a cup of water and blend on high for a minute) or any other type of milk you are partial to

Instructions

Soak the almonds and raisins overnight in filtered water.

In the morning, chop the almonds, and put them in a large cereal bowl. Add all of the raisins, the apple, cinnamon and coconut, and mix with a spoon.

Pour your milk of choice over the top, and enjoy!

You can also experiment with using other nuts and some seeds, of course. I recommend soaking them for a better texture and easier digestion.

# Grapefruit with Mint & Olive Oil

I developed a taste for grapefruit at an early age– we had a tree in our back yard, which kept us in steady supply. It's just one of the fruits I crave most often. We used to cut it in half and eat it with a spoon, but this is really one of the hardest ways you could possibly eat a grapefruit. I think it's so much better to peel and slice it– and this way is prettier, too. When we are having a nice breakfast, I like to make this– the addition of olive oil and salt may seem a little unusual, but I think it really works, smoothing out the grapefruit flavor a bit. (Serves 4)

Ingredients

2 whole grapefruits (I prefer pink)

1 tablespoon finely chopped fresh mint

1 tablespoon extra-virgin olive oil

1/4 teaspoon sea salt (I think a crunchy salt like Maldon sea salt is especially nice here)

a little honey, if needed

Instructions

Cut up the grapefruit. With a serrated knife, cut the ends off the grapefruit, then slice the peel off, from top to bottom, in strips. Cut the fruit in half lengthwise and place on the cutting board cut-side-down. Cut in half again, lengthwise, and then slice across so that you have a lot of triangular slices of grapefruit.

Place the cut fruit into a serving dish, then sprinkle the mint over the top, and drizzle the olive oil. Add the sea salt.

The sweetness of grapefruits can really vary, so taste a piece. If it's too sour or bitter for your tastes, drizzle a little honey over the top before you serve it.

Sides &
Salads

Although I thoroughly appreciate the virtues of a "one pot meal," I think that bringing a few easy bits to the table can dramatically improve the whole affair. In the Philippines, most meals included several dishes, even if they were small, and this manner of creating an abundant spread even for simple meals has stuck with me.

I try to always keep some sauces and condiments on hand, and love throwing together a raw vegetable side to go with the main parts of the meal. This elevates it all-- it's fun to have many flavors, textures and colors on your plate. That said, I don't believe in slaving over weeknight meals. So I have a few tricks up my sleeve for adding interest quickly and easily with these sides, and the sauces and condiments in the next chapter.

A big hurdle a lot of people encounter with going grain-free is what to serve instead of staples like rice, bread, noodles, etc. Hopefully I can provide you with a slew of seriously delicious options that your family will love.

# Cauliflower Rice: 3 Different Ways

My family loves Cauliflower Rice. It's such a perfect and versatile side for so many dishes, and it takes so little time to get it going. There are a few different methods out there for making cauliflower rice, but after quite a bit of experimentation, I have some strong opinions about how it should be done!

Before we get started, I just want to tell you that pre-prepping Cauliflower Rice is a great idea, and one of the major time-savers that I use each week. I typically take two or three heads of cauliflower after we bring home our week's worth of groceries, and then get them all chopped and ready to use during the week.

The recipe below will be for one head of cauliflower, but I recommend a bigger batch, just for the sake of saving time and energy!

## Ingredients

1 head of cauliflower, cut roughly into florets

1 medium yellow onion, cut into quarters

1 tablespoon cooking fat– coconut oil, beef tallow, ghee, bacon grease– you choose!

1 teaspoon sea salt

1 tablespoon fresh lemon juice

a food processor (seriously recommended, although you could do this with a knife and cutting board)

## Instructions

Put your onion into the food processor and chop it finely. Add your roughly chopped cauliflower to the food processor. Process only until uniformly chopped– you don't want to get it too fine, and may have to remove that one last chunk that doesn't seem to want to submit to the blades. (Once you have it chopped evenly, you can store it in a glass container or a ziplock bag to use throughout the week.)

Heat some oil in a medium pot or cast iron skillet. I like to use coconut oil or beef drippings.
Add the cauliflower and onion mixture, and stir it up.

Keep the pan HOT. Make it kind of like a stir fry. (A lot of people steam their cauliflower rice, and this makes me crazy because it gets soggy, and no one likes soggy rice.) Squeeze in some lemon juice and add salt and pepper, stir it around and let it keep cooking until it's tender but still just a little "toothsome." You can put a lid on it briefly if it doesn't seem to be getting tender, but keep an eye on it.

Taste and season. Enjoy!

# 3 Flavor Options

Cauliflower Rice is great just plain, but I often like to add even more presence to mine, and choose a flavor profile that will complement my main dish.

1. Adding cumin works really well for Indian, Middle Eastern, Latin American and Mediterranean food. Add 1 teaspoon whole cumin seeds to the oil in the pan as it heats and let them sizzle for a minute. When it becomes fragrant, add the rice mixture and cook as usual. I make it this way to go with Chelo Kebabs (page 78).

2. For extra color, add turmeric. You will get a neon-yellow rice with a slightly earthy flavor. Add 1/2 teaspoon of ground turmeric to the oil in the pan as it heats and let it sizzle for a minute. When it becomes fragrant, add the rice mixture and cook as usual.

3. For Mexican Cauliflower Rice, add the cumin seeds as described in step one, and then add 1/3 cup tomato puree with the cauliflower mixture. You probably won't need to add more acid, but a little lime juice would taste great. Topping with chopped fresh cilantro at the end is perfect.

There are a hundred and one ways that you can customize your Cauliflower Rice. This is what I love about it– you can make a big bag to keep in your fridge each week, then tweak each batch a little to go with your main dish. Enjoy!

# Turmeric Roasted Potatoes

Potatoes are one the those wonderful foods that you can create all sorts of deliciousness with. I love them steamed, boiled, fried (in beef tallow!) and sautéed. And what I *really* love to make with them is turmeric roasted potatoes– which includes steaming and roasting. And butter. This is a family favorite, and although it takes more than one step to make, it's still quick and easy– well worth your efforts.

These potatoes end up tasting kind of cheesy, and they are total comfort food. I love that the turmeric adds such a wonderful color to an otherwise bland-looking vegetable, and of course turmeric is also a wonderful thing to add into your life anyway– it's a powerful anti-inflammatory with an earthy flavor. You can also add some herbs to your potatoes before roasting– thyme or rosemary are my favorite additions. (Serves 6)

## Ingredients

2 lbs. or 1 kg waxy potatoes

2 teaspoons sea salt

1/4 cup good unsalted butter

1 tablespoon fresh lemon juice

1 teaspoon ground turmeric

a dash cayenne powder, optional

As for kitchen equipment, you'll need a pot with a lid and two handles and then either a baking sheet or an oven-proof serving dish.

## Instructions

Fill your pot about half full with water, and add 1 teaspoon of the salt. Turn heat on high, and bring to a boil.

Peel your potatoes, and cut into quarters. If you have some potatoes that are smaller, just cut in half or leave as they are– you just want to have potato pieces that are roughly the same size.

Once the water is boiling, add your potatoes, and reduce the heat so the water will be at a simmer. Cook until potatoes are just tender, then drain the water completely.

Add the butter, lemon juice, turmeric, and cayenne to the potatoes.

Replace the lid on your pot, and using two oven mitts, shake vigorously. This roughs up the edges of the potatoes while mixing the other ingredients in, making it so you have more surface area for a nice crunchy texture when you roast them. When you open the pot, if the seasonings are not evenly distributed, stir it gently with a spoon.

Turn the potatoes out onto a baking sheet or your oven-proof serving dish. Be sure to scrape out any creamy potatoes inside the pot. Broil your potatoes at 400° F (200° C) until they are getting brown and bubbly on top, about 10 minutes or so.

# Roasted Sweet Potato Puree
# with Ginger, Orange & Coconut

There are not too many dishes that I make the same every year at Thanksgiving, but these sweet potatoes are so good that I don't see any point in making them any other way. This is vegetable candy at its best, without the need for any marshmallow nonsense. This dish is also great for guests that have some food restrictions– they are vegan and absolutely delicious. The magic in this recipe comes from roasting the tubers until they are incredibly sweet and caramelized. (Serves 10)

Ingredients

4 lbs. sweet potatoes

1/2 of a 14 oz. can coconut milk

juice and zest of 1 orange, preferably organic

1 inch fresh ginger, grated

sea salt and pepper to taste

Equipment: either an immersion blender or a food processor.

Instructions

Roast your sweet potatoes in a 350° F or 180° C oven, until they are thoroughly soft. The amount of time will depend completely on the size and thickness of your sweet potatoes, so it will take at least 30 minutes, and could be quite a bit longer.

Remove your sweet potatoes from the oven, and let them cool enough that you can handle them. Pull the skins off and discard– put the roasted sweet potatoes in a large bowl, or in the work bowl of your food processor, if using.

Add the coconut milk, orange juice, ginger and 1 teaspoon of sea salt, and blend– either with immersion blender or food processor– until completely smooth and creamy.

Taste and adjust seasoning as needed.

If making ahead, pour into a baking dish and cover and refrigerate, reheating in a 275° F (140° C) oven before serving.

# Celeriac & Apple Puree

Have you cooked with celeriac before? I think that this root is often passed over for other more familiar vegetables, since it looks so weird. I never really knew what to do with it when I saw it once in a while in the USA, but when we moved to Germany a few years ago, I kept seeing it at the local markets, and decided it was time to give it a try. I am so glad I did-- this root has become one of my family's staples. My favorite way to use celeriac is in a nice mash or purée. It's really simple if you have an immersion blender, and is very easy to adapt to include other vegetables. (Serves 6)

Ingredients

a medium-to-large whole celeriac bulb, peeled

one or two apples

⅓ cup butter

1 tablespoon lemon juice

salt and pepper to taste

Instructions

Roughly chop or slice the whole celeriac bulb, and put it in a pot filled with about an inch of water. Turn the heat under the pot up to medium, put the lid on, and let it steam for about 15 minutes. While it's steaming, peel and chop a large apple (or two). Add the apple after about 15 minutes, and continue steaming (check and add a little more water, if needed) until the celeriac and apple are both very tender.

Drain any remaining liquid from the pot. Add about 1/3 cup of butter (you can add more later, if you'd like), a squeeze of fresh lemon juice, a bit of salt, and some pepper.

Puree this with your immersion blender until fairly smooth.

Taste it. I used a tart apple, and still felt the need for a little more lemon juice. Adjust your seasonings until it tastes how you like it, and then blend some more.

You can serve this just like mashed potatoes. I also enjoy the combination of carrots and celeriac, or turnips and celeriac-- it's hard to go wrong!

# Brussels Sprout Hash

As much as I love cooking for others, I look forward to the chance to make myself lunch or dinner sometimes– when I am cooking for my own appetite alone, not worrying about what other people will want, like, or need. A cheesy brussels sprout hash may not be a satisfactory dinner for my family, but for me, it's perfect. When I am alone, I like to make this and have it with a glass of wine, staring out the window as I eat.

I'm not saying that my family doesn't like it. They do very much, in fact. When they are home, however, this dish is not a main meal, but a side dish. It's excellent that way, too. And if it's not a main meal, then you can certainly leave off the gruyere cheese, and customize it to go with the flavors of the rest of the meal, adding herbs and spices to complement the main attraction. (Serves 4-6)

Ingredients

1 pound brussels sprouts

1 onion, thinly sliced

2 tablespoons bacon grease or ghee

2 tablespoons lemon juice

1/4 teaspoon sea salt

1/8 teaspoon freshly ground black pepper

1/2 cup grated gruyere cheese (optional)

a food processor will make this much easier, and you'll need a cast iron skillet

Instructions

Cut the stems from the brussels sprouts and use a food processor to shred them. Alternatively, you can slice each in half, then cut each half into thin slices, about 1/8 inch thick.

Heat the bacon grease or ghee in a cast iron skillet over high heat for about a minute– you want it hot! Add the onions and brussels sprouts.

Stir-fry, moving around with a spatula, until the sprouts are bright green– about three minutes.

Add the lemon juice, salt and pepper and cook for 1 additional minute.

Taste and adjust seasonings.

If using cheese, turn your oven broiler on to high, and sprinkle the cheese over the top of the hash. Pop the skillet in under the boiler, and cook until the cheese is bubbly and golden.

There are so many great ways to mix this hash up and turn it into a full meal. A favorite is to chop up some bacon and fry it in the skillet first, then remove the meat and fry the brussels sprouts and add it back in later with the cheese. Another family favorite is to use Thanksgiving leftovers– add turkey and some sage, and then at the end add some fresh cranberries and cook briefly for a tangy pop. We literally made that about five times in a row last year, we loved it so much.

# Roasted Pepper & Eggplant Gazpacho

I have long been a huge fan of gazpacho. It's just so fresh, and the flavors– to me– are the essence of summer. Although it's not traditional to have eggplant in this Spanish cold soup, I think it works beautifully as a replacement for the stale bread in most recipes. It thickens the soup really nicely, and adds a great flavor.

Ingredients

one medium-sized eggplant

4-6 medium-sized tomatoes

2 sweet red peppers

3 cloves garlic, skin on

1 small bunch parsley

2 tablespoons red wine vinegar or sherry vinegar

1/4 cup extra-virgin olive oil

sea salt

black pepper

1/2 cup diced cucumber

in terms of equipment, you will need a blender or a food processor, and a baking sheet

Instructions

Wash your veggies, and slice the eggplant into quarters. Slice your tomatoes and peppers in half. Place the eggplant, tomatoes, peppers and garlic cloves on a baking sheet, with the vegetables skin-side up.

Roast under the broiler on high heat. When the tomato skins begin to char, remove them with tongs and put in the blender. Rotate peppers and eggplant if needed, to get the skins to roast more or less evenly. If something is looking pretty brown and bubbly, take it out and add it to the blender. Once everything is roasted, take the skin off of the garlic, and pour the veggies and any juice that has accumulated in the pan into the blender.

Blend the vegetables until smooth. Reserve a few sprigs of the parsley, and roughly chop the rest, including the stems, and add to the blender. Add the red wine vinegar, olive oil, and salt and pepper to taste. Blend again, and taste. Adjust seasonings– especially salt and vinegar. Add some water if the soup is too thick, and keep in mind that it will thicken a bit more as it cools.

Chill in the fridge, then garnish with the diced cucumber, some parsley and a drizzle of olive oil when it's time to serve. Enjoy!


P.S. This gazpacho also makes a really nice sauce for zucchini noodles! I love using my spiralizer and adding some roasted chicken for a main meal, or just the sauce as a side dish.

# Spring & Summer Smoked Salmon Salad

This Scandinavian-inspired dish is a newer revelation. I love the pretty colors and coolness of it all. It's ideal for a hot summer day, but I have to mention the fact that it showcases so many springtime vegetables-- so it's great for either season. I plan to make this part of the next brunch I serve. (Serves 4 as a main, or 8 as an appetizer)

Ingredients

5 new potatoes, cut into quarters

one large head of crispy romaine lettuce

1/4 cup chopped flat leaf parsley

5 radishes, thinly sliced

3 ripe tomatoes-- only use if in season!

several rings of thinly sliced red onion, either pickled (page 71) or soaked in vinegar for a few minutes

6 ounces of smoked salmon

Creamy Lemon & Dill Salad Dressing (page 64)

Instructions

Begin by boiling the quartered potatoes in a pot of salted water until barely tender. Then run cold water over them to cool to room temperature.

Layer the salad ingredients (in order, starting with the lettuce) on a large serving platter.

Arrange the potato slices and tomatoes around the sides.

Serve the Creamy Lemon & Dill Salad Dressing on the side.

Enjoy!

# Fennel & Orange Salad

I'd like to share my family's favorite salad. It is really simple, but the combination of flavors works so well that the resulting dish is greater than the sum of its parts. I love fennel– it's so fresh and sweet, and leaves such a clean taste in your mouth. Fennel and orange go really well together, and I love this non-traditional salad.

This recipe is the perfect, fresh side dish for just about any meal– but particularly in the summertime. I love to serve it alongside Chelo Kebabs (page 78) or Greek Lamb Kebabs (page 87)– and last night we had it with our grilled Spatchcock Chicken (page 74). We have never made it without having the dish disappear quickly– definitely no leftovers here!  (Serves 4)

Ingredients

1 large or 2 small fresh bulbs of fennel

2 small (or one large) oranges

2 tablespoons extra-virgin olive oil

1 tablespoon of orange juice (fresh lemon juice will also work)

salt (I like to use Maldon sea salt for this)

freshly cracked pepper

1/4 cup flat leaf parsley, chopped

Instructions

Thinly slice the bulb of fennel, as high up as you can before you get to the fronds. A mandoline is awesome for this job, but if you don't have one, then you can just slice the bulb very thinly with a good chef's knife. Slice horizontally across the bottom, so you'll get little crescent shaped slices of fennel. Put these on the serving dish.

Peel and slice the orange with a sharp knife. Start by cutting off the top and bottom portion of the orange, and then work around slicing off the peel in vertical strips until the orange is bare.

Cut that in half vertically, then break it down into thick little wedges. Put the orange slices on top of the fennel.

Drizzle the olive oil over the top, apply the salt and pepper, and then squeeze a little bit of orange over– this is your "dressing."

Top with the chopped parsley, and serve.

Enjoy! I think you will love having this salad alongside dinner on warm summery evenings. It's also a great side for a nice brunch!

# Strawberry Bruschetta Relish

Strawberries are one of those foods that I wait eagerly for through the cold months of the year. A strawberry is the essence of summer, and one of my favorite foods in the world. Tomatoes and basil also embody the spirit of summer to me, and so I think it's perfect to combine the three. Living in Los Angeles with an abundance of tomatoes and basil for most of the year, I made bruschetta constantly-- it's so fresh and versatile. It goes great on eggs, grilled salmon or halibut, and makes a perfect salad dressing, too.

If I ever get a disappointingly tart batch of strawberries, turning them into a bruschetta relish is my first move. Balsamic vinegar sweetens everything up, and the acidity is just right alongside tomatoes. (Makes 2 cups)

Ingredients

1 cup chopped and seeded sweet tomatoes– cherry or grape tomatoes are great for this. One variety than I can always rely on to be sweet (even if I'm making it out of season) is Roma.

1 cup washed and quartered strawberries

1 medium bunch of basil (about 1/4 cup packed) chopped into ribbons

3 tablespoons extra-virgin olive oil

2 tablespoons balsamic vinegar

1 clove of garlic, crushed under a knife blade (You can chop yours finely if you love garlic, but I prefer the gentle infusion of flavor without the bite of raw garlic in each mouthful.)

salt and pepper to taste

Instructions

Combine all of the ingredients in a medium-sized bowl, and gently toss until evenly mixed.

Add freshly cracked pepper and salt to taste, and add more balsamic vinegar, if needed.

Try not to eat all of it straight out of the bowl before you can give some other people a chance to enjoy it.

This relish is so good spooned atop poached or gently-fried eggs, as a side salad, or as a relish for grilled fish. And you should definitely know that leftovers can be blended up with some added vinegar and olive oil for a truly fantastic Strawberry Balsamic Salad Dressing.

# Chocolate Black Beans
## with Oranges & Cinnamon

Have you had Chocolate Black Beans before? If not, you are in for a big treat. This is my favorite way to prepare beans to go with Mexican or other Latin American food. I enjoyed so much amazing Latin American food in Los Angeles, and I honestly can't remember where I got the idea to add chocolate to my beans— but I think this is inspired by Mexican chocolate moles.

In college, I traveled to Honduras a few times, and the black beans there also made an impression on me— so thick and rich. They were probably cooked with bone broth, a fact that would have horrified my young-and-vegan self. Now I am always thankful to be able to make my beans with bone broths, which makes them extra-nourishing and unctuous.

Oranges and cinnamon add a sweetness that go so nicely with the bittersweet chocolate— and cilantro is a must at the end, for those who enjoy it. (Serves 8)

Ingredients

2 cups dry black beans, soaked overnight or at least 8 hours in fresh water

2 tablespoons bacon fat, beef drippings or ghee

1 large onion, diced

1 tablespoon cumin (can be seeds or powder)

1 teaspoon cinnamon

1/2 teaspoon smoked paprika (optional)

4- 6 cups bone broth (chicken or beef) or water

1/4 cup chopped or about 50g bittersweet chocolate bar

juice of one orange

juice of one lime (optional)

salt and pepper to taste

one small bunch cilantro, chopped fine

Instructions

Drain and rinse the black beans.

Heat the fat in a heavy-bottomed pot with a lid, and add the onions. Sauté until translucent, then add the spices and fry gently with the onions until fragrant.

Add the black beans and broth (or water). Add enough liquid to cover the beans by half an inch. Add the chocolate, stir, and bring to the boil. Reduce to a simmer and cook until beans are starting to become tender. Add the orange juice, salt and pepper. (Just a tip— don't add salt to beans before they are tender, because it causes the outside to harden, and it will take forever to get them to soften.)

Cook on low heat, stirring occasionally until the beans are beginning to blend with the liquid. Taste and season with more orange juice or some lime juice, and salt. When the beans are done, add the cilantro.

Enjoy! These Chocolate Black Beans are even better the next day, and freeze beautifully.

# Market Days in Bury St. Edmunds

I love shopping at open markets. My very first experience with this was waking up before dawn, and heading out with our cook, Nang Sarah, when I was a little girl in the Philippines. I mostly remember the energy of the market– everyone talking at once, haggling, grabbing fruits and vegetables to assess, weigh, bag and purchase. And, of course there were the **smells**! Dried fish piled high, fresh seafood being cleaned, and every other kind of meat being butchered to order.

I learned by observation, to look closely at what was being offered, to find the best quality and prices, and to be a keen and loyal buyer. I have actually never lived in a place that did not have open markets. In my early twenties in California, I arranged my whole work and school schedule around going to the Whittier farmer's market. I loved seeing the same people each week, developing those connections with the vendors, and learning about my food.

In Germany, this was one of the first ways I integrated into regular life in Amberg. I went to the market square several times each week to shop. I had to speak German, and so my food vocabulary grew faster than anything else. It didn't take long for vendors to start to recognize me, and they were so kind about my weak, apprehensive *Deutsch*. It felt so good to me to be going about life just like the people around me, buying ingredients for that night's dinner, and discovering food items that were unique to the region.

I know that shopping frequently is really unusual (and probably seems crazy to many) in the USA. Most families shop as little as possible, stocking up their cupboards, fridges and freezers. That's just not what I am used to, and it feels good to me to shop often, planning my meals each day around what looks best.

Farmers markets are making a comeback in England. Most areas have had them for about ten years, at the most. Bury St. Edmunds is considered a market town, because they have two markets each week. Unlike the typical markets in the US (or Germany, in my experience) these have a lot more going on than fresh produce. There are people selling pretty much anything you can think of– clothes, books, home repair items, dog beds, fabric and notions, vacuum cleaners… The feeling is definitely different from the sort of country-bliss scene you might expect in a place like Suffolk. The other thing is that *most* of the produce is *not local*! Much of it is imported from places like Greece, Turkey, Spain, and even China. And it is cheap– in quality and price.

It was fairly easy to pick out the two vendors that were selling mainly local produce, and they are the ones I buy from each week. There is also a really good fish monger, and we try to have a seafood meal once or twice a week.

And, at last, we have an *organic* farm selling at our market! This is a really big deal. Plus, they carry heirloom varieties, and lots of greens– something I have found conspicuously absent here, with the exception of cabbages. Yes, their produce costs more. But it is *worth* more. I try to buy as much as I possibly can from them, after carefully considering the most economical way to do so. They have the most incredible salad greens right now, which are a tart and peppery blend of arugula, sorrel, mizuna, frisee, miners lettuce, and mustard greens. And they are one of the only ones selling fresh herbs (really surprising, right?).

So now I enjoy the busy market days more than ever. It's a nice time to be out with the rest of the town. English people do tend to keep to themselves, so this is one venue where I can participate in town life, chat with the vendors who all recognize me now, and are happy to see me, amazingly enough!

I'm so glad for our market! I consider myself lucky to live in a "market town" here in England, and do not take access to fresh, organic produce for granted.

Dips, Sauces & Condiments

I love making my own sauces and condiments. Most are easy to put together, and keep for a long time in the fridge. This means that I can cook up a super simple meal, and then have some amazing, bright flavors to add in at the end. Taking the time to whip some up actually makes cooking much easier overall.

If you have been buying all of your salad dressings, dips, and sauces, then I think you are in for a wonderful surprise: **yours will taste better.** Using really fresh ingredients and blending them to your own tastes is really empowering. And you'll save money too, of course!

# Babaganoush

Babaganoush is a summertime staple at our house.  This is one of my favorite dips of all time.  It's rich and full of flavor, and goes well with raw veggie sticks, grilled eggplant slices, chips, and as a side to a Middle Eastern meal.  It also freezes well, so this is a great option for using up summer produce. (Makes about 2 cups)

## Ingredients

3 medium eggplants (about 2 pounds total)

2 cloves of garlic, minced, or 4-5 cloves of roasted garlic* (my preference, see note below)

2 tablespoons juice from 1 lemon, plus more as needed

3 tablespoons tahini

1 teaspoon ground cumin

1/4 teaspoon smoked paprika (optional)

a dash (or more) of cayenne pepper (optional)

1/3 cup extra-virgin olive oil

1/4 cup chopped fresh parsley or cilantro leaves

sea salt

fresh pepper

*There are lots of more complicated ways to roast garlic, but I just throw a whole head of it into the oven while I'm broiling the eggplant. It gets soft, and the flavor mellows and deepens.

## Instructions

Cut the eggplants in half, length-wise and roast under a broiler, flipping halfway through.  They need to be well-browned on each side, and smooshy all over.  Bonus points: Grill over a fire, for a nice, smoky flavor.

Place the eggplant in a medium-sized mixing bowl.  Let it cool (seriously!) and then peel the skin off.  I sometimes leave *a little* bit of charred skin on for flavor.  Some liquid will pool in the bowl– don't pour it off– it's sweet and delicious!

Add the spices, 2 tablespoons of lemon juice, the tahini and olive oil, and the fresh herbs to the bowl.

I use an immersion blender to blend it all really smooth.  Of course you could use a regular blender or a food processor.  I have often made this just with a fork, a nice chunky version– naturally, you would need to chop the ingredients pretty thoroughly first if you go that route.

Taste and season (does it need more salt, more of a little kick from cayenne, is the tartness about right?).

Transfer to a serving bowl and drizzle with a little olive oil and garnish with chopped herbs.

# Creamy Stinging Nettles Dip
# with Roasted Garlic & Mint

Do you have stinging nettles in your area? This plant has a bad reputation because it can hurt you. But the thing is, it can also really nourish you and take care of you, if you know how to use it. I never noticed them in my landscapes (although I'm sure they were there) until I moved to England. They are *everywhere* here, and now that I know what to do with them, I think I'm very lucky.

One of my favorite things to do with stinging nettles is to turn them into a dip. And my favorite flavors to combine them with are roasted garlic and fresh mint, along with some tangy Greek yogurt. This is really easy to make, and is so fresh and delicious. We like to eat ours with cucumber slices, or heaped onto slices of grilled eggplant, or used as a sauce like Greek tatziki. (Makes 2 cups)

Ingredients

1 cup blanched stinging nettles

2 tablespoon extra virgin olive oil

5 cloves roasted garlic* or one clove fresh garlic

1/4 cup fresh mint leaves

1 tablespoon fresh lemon juice

a dash of cayenne pepper, or more to taste

1 teaspoon sea salt, plus more to taste

3/4 cup Greek yogurt (sour cream will also work)

In terms of equipment, you will need a food processor, or a blender, plus a silicone spatula.

* Roast garlic by wrapping a whole head in foil and slowly baking it in the oven until soft. If you want the roasted garlic flavor but don't have the time, you can <u>slowly</u> cook some sliced garlic in olive oil in a skillet, and use that instead.

Instructions

Put the nettles into the food processor and blend until roughly chopped.

Add the rest of the ingredients and blend until smooth. (Note: I usually blend before adding the Greek yogurt so I can set some aside for my dairy-intolerant daughter. Then I blend in the yogurt for the rest of us.)

Taste and adjust seasoning. The two things I always look for are whether I need to add a little more acid (lemon juice) or salt.

# Foraging For Nettles

If you think that gathering stinging nettles is not your cup of tea, I really hope to change your mind. Nettles are one of the first things that can be foraged, at the first sign of spring, and they are extremely plentiful. Stinging nettle has a long list of health-enhancing properties, and is good for eating, drinking, and use as a medicinal tonic (both internally and externally).
The stems of the plant have also traditionally been used for making fibers– twine and linen-like materials. *And to think that we generally regard them as weeds!*

A couple of winters ago, we went on our first nettle foraging outing, and we have been hooked ever since. After a couple days of mild weather in late February, we thought that maybe there might be some nettles making their appearance nearby. We all grabbed thick gloves, scissors or clippers, bags and baskets, and headed out to our nearby greenways. I really wondered if we might be too early, but it was nice to get out for a walk, and the end of winter has such a unique beauty. Plus, it's always exciting to spot some of the first signs of spring!

There were nettles growing back, after all. At first, I was a little unsure, since there were so many varieties growing together. I did a quick google search to make sure that everything was nettle, and of course did the old *sting test* on myself as well. Sure enough! We've all been stung by nettles before, and it does really hurt. Amelia has become an expert at identifying them. I had stopped to point them out to her many times last year, but it wasn't until she put her face into a bunch to smell them that she really developed an eye for the plant! No problems ever since, as you might imagine! We were all gloved and wearing long sleeves, so besides my voluntary test and a couple other minor pricks, no one got hurt.

We were good foragers, and only snipped the tops off of about 10% of each section we found. It took a long time to gather the amount we were after, but it couldn't have been more pleasant! There were clusters of snowdrops, warty tree trunks, and algae-coated swamps. I loved seeing the remains of last summer's eager foliage. And watching my two favorite people hunt for food.
As if having two bags stuffed full of nettles wasn't enough, we had a wonderful visit with a flock of very friendly sheep on our way home. I think they wanted some of our bounty.

We weighed our nettles when we got home, and they reached almost a kilogram. That is a really good amount! Stings were minimal, and we all had such a relaxing afternoon. I started making Nettles Beer when we got home.

After I used the nettles for the beer-making tea, I also pureed the greens and made a really wonderful Stinging Nettles Dip with Roasted Garlic & Mint (page 54)– it was a gorgeous deep emerald color, and was so delicious. Nettles are a new favorite over here!

# Herbed Compound Butter

Compound butter is one of those "secret weapons" I try to have in the fridge or freezer at all times. I first came across it at a favorite restaurant, where they were serving it just to spread on their homemade bread. I love to add a pat to steak. It's great on fish, and can be used to rub under the chicken skin before roasting a chicken, too. I like to put it on steamed vegetables, and it works as a nice little butter sauce on just about anything. You could also add it to the pan before sautéing mushrooms, or even making scrambled eggs. This is one of those things that has as many uses as you can think of! The variations on this theme are also unlimited.

Here's a simple version, and you can switch out the herbs, spices and acids to make new combinations.

Ingredients

1 lb. butter

small bunch fresh parsley (or other lively herb)

2 tablespoons lemon juice

1 tablespoon cumin seed

1 teaspoon sea salt

1 tablespoon olive oil

1/2 teaspoon fresh ground pepper

dash cayenne pepper (optional)

Instructions

Put all ingredients into a small food processor and blend. Scrape down the sides as needed, until everything is evenly incorporated.

You can store this by putting the butter in a glass container, or by rolling it into a log in parchment paper, cutting slices off when you need it. It will keep for about two weeks in the fridge.

# Tahini Sauce

This is a condiment I make every single week (sometimes more than once) without fail. It goes great on so many things, and can be whipped up in literally one minute, once you know the basics. Add a good glug of olive oil and a little extra water, and it turns into a great, creamy salad dressing!

Ingredients

½ cup of tahini paste

juice of ½ lemon

½ teaspoon salt

1 dash of cayenne powder

3 tablespoons of very cold water

Instructions

Combine the first four ingredients in a bowl, and whisk gently to mix.

Add the cold water (put an ice cube in it if you need to-- the cold temperature makes the sauce thick and creamy!) and whisk well, until thick and creamy. You can add a little more water if it's too thick.

Taste and adjust seasoning-- you may want a little more salt, lemon juice or cayenne. Make it how you like it.

This will store in a sealed jar for about 5 days.

# Fruit Vinegars

This is a really easy project that will give you a wonderful, unique vinegar for your salads.

If you are enjoying a bunch of strawberries, plums, cherries, etc., or making jam or other fruity projects, don't just throw away the tops, pits and scraps! Collect them in a clean jar, then cover them with apple cider vinegar or white wine vinegar. Let them steep in the cupboard for about a week. When you strain them out, you will have a gorgeous bottle of Fruit Vinegar!

It's great for putting on salads, or adding to cocktails.

I made this Strawberry Vinegar last year, and it was really nice. I also did the same with cherry pits, which produced an even stronger flavor– so good!

# Pumpkin Seed & Apple Vinaigrette Dressing

I always think of Germany when I make this one. I loved shopping for food in Amberg– the prices were fantastic, and the quality was great, and there were always really pleasant surprises on those market shelves. The *Netto Mart* a few doors down from our apartment was so tiny, but had all kinds of good stuff on the shelves, including bottles of inexpensive *Kürbiskenöl*– pumpkin seed oil! I loved making salads with greens, sliced apples, toasted sesame seeds, some farmer's cheese, all tossed in this vinaigrette.

Whenever I can get my hands on pumpkin seed oil now, I use it to make this dressing, and we all think of our autumn in Germany.

Ingredients

1 tablespoon apple cider vinegar

1/2 small shallot, peeled and roughly chopped

1/2 teaspoon dijon mustard

4 tablespoons pumpkin seed oil

1/8 teaspoon sea salt

a couple grinds of black pepper

you will need an immersion blender or a regular blender, or you can just chop the shallots *very* finely and shake in a jar

Instructions

Put all ingredients into the cylinder work bowl for an immersion blender and process until creamy. (You can do this in a standard blender, as well-- but will need to double or triple the recipe so there is enough bulk to flow around the blades properly.)
This will store well in a jar in the fridge for at least a week.

# Classic French Vinaigrette Dressing

This vinaigrette is made at least weekly in our house.  It's the perfect quick dressing for a fresh green salad (preferably with very thinly sliced radishes in it) and to marinate warm, boiled leeks for a wonderful side dish.  (Makes about 1/3 cup)

Ingredients

1/8 teaspoon sea salt

1 tablespoon white wine vinegar

1/2 small shallot, peeled and roughly chopped

1/2 teaspoon dijon mustard

3- 4 tablespoons olive oil

you will need an immersion blender or a regular blender

Instructions

Put all ingredients into the cylinder work bowl for an immersion blender and process until creamy. (You can do this in a standard blender, as well-- but will need to double or triple the recipe so there is enough bulk to flow around the blades properly.)

Taste and adjust the seasonings to your liking. Store in a tightly sealed glass bottle in the fridge-- it will last for up to a week.

# Karen's Spanish Vinaigrette

This recipe comes from an American expat friend of mine, passed down from her Spanish mother-in-law. She brought a salad to an expat Thanksgiving dinner we hosted last year, along with a little jar of dressing. I don't remember the salad, but I had thirds just so I could enjoy more of this dressing!
It is very simple, and we have been making it at least once a week ever since then. (Makes 1/2 cup)

Ingredients

2 tablespoons balsamic or red wine vinegar

1/3 cup extra-virgin olive oil

1 clove of garlic, smashed

1/4 teaspoon salt, maybe more

a grind of fresh pepper

you can make this in a jar with a lid

Instructions

Put all of these ingredients into a jar with a tight lid.  Shake vigorously until blended.

And that's it!

Karen makes it really salty, and I like that.  So after you taste it for the first time, you might try adding an extra pinch of salt to see how you like that.

# Creamy Lemon & Dill Dressing

This dressing was a new one I came up with this summer– and then proceeded to whip up over and over again. It's so simple, but genuinely wonderful. I will go ahead and tell you that it makes an unbelievably light potato salad (if that is even possible) with simply boiled potatoes.
(Makes 2/3 cup)

Ingredients

1/2 cup cultured heavy cream-- sour cream, crème fraîche, or even Greek yogurt will work in
a pinch

the zest and juice of half of an unwaxed,
organic lemon

1/4 cup chopped fresh dill

salt and pepper to taste

Instructions

Whisk all of the ingredients together.

Taste and adjust seasoning. If it's too thick, you can thin it out with a little water.

Try not to eat it as a "chilled soup." Or, go ahead! But make a double batch next time, so you'll have enough for your salad.

# Roasted Tomatillo Salsa

When the weather turns warm, I get a lot of hankerings for Central American.  Whenever I find tomatillos at the organic stand at our local market, I first take a moment to celebrate quietly, and then I make them into this: Roasted Tomatillo Salsa.  It's so easy and good– you can probably go from ingredients to salsa in 10-15 minutes flat.

Lately I've been making Chocolate Black Beans (page 46), Carne Asada (page 94), and this Roasted Tomatillo Salsa.  It tastes like home (Los Angeles) to me, and makes me pretty happy.

Ingredients

about a dozen tomatillos, husks removed

3-4 medium tomatoes

two onions, cut into quarters

a hot chile, cut in half– optional

2 limes

one small bunch (about 1/4 cup packed) cilantro

salt and pepper

In terms of equipment, a blender or food processor is perfect, plus a baking sheet you can put under your oven broiler.

Instructions

Cut the tomatillos and tomatoes in half, and place cut-side down on the baking sheet.

Arrange the onions on the pan as well, and the chile, if using.

Place the baking sheet under your oven broiler, on full blast.  Broil until the veggies are turning brown and bubbly.  You may want to turn the onions with some kitchen tongs, for more even cooking– but no need to move the tomatoes around, and that will just get messy.  Remove the tomatoes and tomatillos a little earlier than the onions, to let the onions brown a bit more.  This should all take about 10 minutes or so.

Put all of the roasted veggies into your blender or food processor, add a teaspoon of salt and the juice of one of the lemons, plus the cilantro, and blend until smooth.

Taste your salsa and adjust the seasoning by increasing lime juice and salt as needed, until the flavor is balanced.

Enjoy!

# Chimichurri Sauce

I love Chimichurri Sauce. It's bold, bright, and herbal. The main thing I use it for is to top a quickly-grilled flank steak (page 155). This makes a phenomenal meal in just a few minutes. This recipe also works as a meat marinade, great for chicken, beef, and lamb alike. (Makes about a cup of sauce)

Ingredients

1 cup firmly packed fresh flat-leaf parsley

2 garlic cloves

2 tablespoons fresh oregano (or 2 teaspoons dried oregano)

1 teaspoon sea salt

2-4 tablespoons olive oil (start with two, add more if you think it needs more liquid)

2 tablespoons white wine vinegar (red or apple cider vinegar will also work here)

1/4 teaspoon freshly ground black pepper

1/4-1/2 teaspoon red pepper flakes

Instructions

Put all ingredients into a small food processor and process until everything is chopped fine and blended, scraping down the sides as needed.

Taste and adjust seasonings. Either freeze leftovers in ice cube trays, or keep in a sealed jar in the fridge where it will last for a week.

# Pontack Sauce (Elderberry Ketchup)

Pontack Sauce is a traditional English condiment. What I love about this sauce is that it doesn't have any added sugar, it keeps forever, and has a nice tangy flavor reminiscent of Worcestershire Sauce– but with berries. It's fairly simple to make, and goes really well with game meats. The way we use it most is as a steak sauce.

This is a recipe adapted from two different versions, found in Food DIY and River Cottage Preserves. If you have elderberries in your area, or you can get them dried, I hope you'll try making this sauce. I can't help thinking that a version of this made with cherries would also be wonderful...

Ingredients

2 pounds fresh elderberries, or 12 ounces dried elderberries

4 cups apple cider vinegar (white wine vinegar will also work)

1 pound shallots, minced

10 whole cloves

10 allspice berries

1 tablespoon freshly grated ginger

2 tablespoons cracked black peppercorns

1 teaspoon salt

Instructions

Using a fork, strip the berries from their stems. The stems are toxic, so do your best to remove as much as possible.

Put the berries in a dutch oven with a lid. Add the vinegar, and bake in the oven for 4-6 hours at 325°. The smell is really pleasant– more yeasty than vinegar-y, and of course nice and fruity.

Strain the berries out with a sieve, pressing to get all of the juice. Return the juice to your dutch oven or to a sauce pan.

Add the shallots and spices to the elderberry juice, and bring to a boil over medium heat on the stove. Reduce heat and let simmer for 25 minutes. Strain out the shallots and spices, and bring to the boil again, for five minutes.

Bottle your sauce into sterilized glass vessels. I use glass bottles.

Give it time to mature. Right after it's done, the shallot flavor is quite sharp. This will mellow and the sauce improves over time– years, even. This is shelf-stable for many, many years, so take your time.

# Pickled & Perfumed Pink Onions

After I made these pickled onions for the first time, I proceeded to repeat the process over and over and over again, while we consumed huge quantities with every meal. Sometimes that's just how it is with food. Naturally, we burned out after a few weeks. Now we're back to a more normal pace with these, and they are truly wonderful-- and ridiculously simple to make. The cardamom and coriander give these onions an almost flowery aroma, making them unlike all of the other pickled onions I've eaten.

I love to add these hot pink onions to salads, burgers, and as a side to Asian food. When you are done with the onions, the remaining vinegar is wonderful, whisked with olive oil, into a pungent, fragrant salad dressing.

## Ingredients

1 large red onion, peeled and sliced into thin rings

4 pods of green cardamom

1/2 teaspoon coriander seeds

4 whole black peppercorns

about 1 cup of apple cider vinegar or white wine vinegar

1/2 teaspoon sea salt

you'll also need a pint-sized glass jar

## Instructions

Put the onion slices in the jar, and add the spices.

Pour over the vinegar until the onions are completely covered.

Seal the jar and leave on your counter for a few hours or even overnight.

Enjoy!

These will keep in the fridge for a week, if you can manage to leave them for that long.

Note that you can use this brine a second time for another batch.

Dinner

Dinnertime is kind of a sacred thing at our house. It's something we make room for every day. We sit down at the table together and take our time eating, talking, and being together. In the wintertime, when the days are short, we read books at the table together, like my family did when I was a kid. Eating meals is a source of joy and pleasure, and so we make it a priority to give ourselves the time and space for good, nourishing, and relaxing meals.

But that doesn't mean that I spend all afternoon in the kitchen. Nope, not at all. The recipes I share with you here are the ones we make all of the time, and don't require hours slaving over the stove. They are easy to prepare, but completely delicious and satisfying.

For me, food and everything surrounding it (growing, buying, preparing, eating) are the best parts of life. I don't believe in rushing through these things– this is the essence of living. We all have to eat, and it is a communal act. How wonderful that having to fuel our bodies is also very pleasurable, and builds community. I derive great satisfaction from buying food from people I trust, and preparing it in my kitchen for the people I love.

# Spatchcock Roasted Chicken

One fine summer day, I asked my butcher for a whole chicken. "Do you want it spatchcocked?" he asked. Before I knew what spatchcocked meant, I said "Yes." Then, I watched him deftly remove the backbone, and splay it out, flat– "See, I like to call it "roadkill chicken," he said with a sly grin. I bought it. And I think he may come to regret ever showing me spatchcock chicken. I love to cook whole chickens– but it takes time, and it's a little tricky to do on the barbecue in the summer (although I have tried and enjoyed the classic beer can chicken). We started buying spatchcock chicken every week, and when the weather is warm, I buy two at a time, since they make such great leftovers.

In order to make this recipe, we'll need to make the marinade, learn to spatchcock a chicken, and then cook it. I've broken each step up for you, but I promise it's actually all pretty simple.

# Garlic, Lemon and Ginger Marinade

## Ingredients

1 small bunch of thyme

4 cloves garlic

1 inch of fresh ginger root, sliced

1 tablespoon sea salt

juice of 1 lemon (about 1/4 cup)

3 tablespoons olive oil

pepper to taste

a dash of cayenne pepper (optional)

## Instructions

Put all ingredients into a small food processor and blend until everything is chopped fine and blended like a salad dressing.

Here's an extra little tip– if garlic is sometimes hard for you to digest, take out the little green stalk that may be growing in the middle– this bit is full of a substance designed to protect it from being eaten in its most tender stage, and this is usually what we are sensitive to.

# Smoky Turmeric Marinade

## Ingredients

3 cloves garlic

1 teaspoon turmeric powder

1/2 teaspoon smoked paprika

1 tablespoon sea salt

juice of 1 lemon (about 1/4 cup)

3 tablespoons melted bacon fat (recommended) or olive oil

1/4 cup chopped cilantro, plus a bit more for garnish

pepper to taste

a dash of cayenne pepper (optional)

## Instructions

Put all ingredients into a small food processor and blend until everything is chopped fine and blended. It will be thicker than a dressing, and a good consistency to rub onto the chicken with your hands.

# How to Spatchcock a Chicken

Spatchcocking is basically splitting open and flattening out a bird for broiling, grilling or barbecuing. This speeds up the cooking time and ensures more even cooking. I also find that it produces a much juicier chicken!

What to do:

1. Put your chicken breast-side-down on a cutting board.

2. Using a sharp knife, remove the backbone from the bird. Start by carefully putting a knife through the bottom-end of the bird until you see the point of the knife emerge at the neck. Push the knife down hard against one side of the spine, cutting through the rib cage. You may need to pull your knife along the spine from the neck to the tail, depending on your knife.

3. Open up the bird and cut away the spine at the other side in the same way.

4. Carve around the breast bone to remove it, and save these trimmed bits for making chicken stock.

5. Now the bird should be nice and flat, for even cooking.

# To Prepare the Chicken

Make either of the marinades.

Put the chicken in a wide glass dish (like a pie pan) pour the marinade over it. Turn it over so both sides get covered. I often make two chickens at a time, laying one on top of the other, marinated, with the insides facing each other. Reserve a little marinade to brush the chicken with as it cooks.

Cover with wax paper or a lid and put the chicken back in the fridge overnight or for at least an hour. Honestly, the marinade is so flavorful that I have had great results with little rest time. But if you have the option, longer is better.

Heat your oven to 450° F (235° C). Put your chicken skin-side-down on an oven rack (with a pan beneath to catch the drips) or use a broiler pan and roast for 20 minutes, or until the meat is turning a delicious golden-brown color. Turn the chicken over. This is kind of tricky– you may need to employ the use of two pairs of tongs, or tongs and spatula. The trick is to move quickly. You'll get better with practice, I promise. Once it's skin-side-up, apply the reserved marinade, and continue roasting until the skin is getting crispy and brown– about 25 minutes. Since the chicken is flat, it cooks much more quickly, and somehow (magically?) retains lots of moisture. Ooh, la la!

When your chicken is ready, take it tenderly out of the oven and let it rest for 10 minutes (you can cover it with tented foil if you don't want to lose too much heat) so the juices don't run out when you cut it up.

Eat it with your fingers. OK, you don't have to. But it's SO good that you will probably want to. The skin is crispy, garlicky and salty with just the right little tang. I like to squeeze some fresh lemon over ours, and add some fresh herb that I used in the marinade for garnish.

# Chelo Kebabs with Cucumber & Yogurt Salad

Our winters in England can be pretty mild, but I still get that intense ache for brighter, longer days. I self-medicate with flavors that come from sunny climes, making foods I associate with summertime. One of my favorites is Chelo Kebabs.

These are super-quick to make, freeze easily, are budget friendly and– most importantly– seriously delicious. We buy ground beef every week, and this is one of those things that I can whip up quickly when I don't know what else to make. A few condiments, olives and some Cauliflower Rice (page 33) round out the meal easily, and we're all happy.

# Chelo Kebab Recipe

This recipe is an adaptation from Ariana Bundy's recipe from her gorgeous cookbook, <u>Pomegranates &</u> <u>Roses</u>. And I will just go ahead and tell you right now that you should double the recipe because these are great as leftovers for lunch! You can slice them up and serve them as finger food (see the photo on page 81) or put them in Greek salads the next day.

## Ingredients

1 medium onion, skinned and cut into quarters

1 lb. (500g) fatty ground beef or lamb (I usually ask my butcher to give me a blend of 75% beef, 25% lamb)

1/4 teaspoon ground turmeric

a generous pinch of baking powder

1 teaspoon salt

a few grinds of fresh black pepper

1 teaspoon dried mint

chopped fresh herbs like coriander (cilantro) or parsley to garnish, optional

chili flakes and ground sumac to garnish, optional

lemon wedges to garnish, optional

Equipment: You will want to use a food processor for this recipe (it's possible to make it without, just a lot more work) and a rimmed baking sheet. Shish kebab skewers are optional.

## Instructions

Put the onion into the food processor and process until finely chopped. Gather the onions to one side of the work bowl and use a paper towel or a clean kitchen towel to press as much liquid out as you can.

Add the meat, salt, spices and baking powder, and process for about 30 seconds to one minute. You want the meat to be smooth and well-blended. This might seem weird, but it works!

Form the meat into kebabs. It will be sticky, and if you want you can dip your fingers into a bowl of cold water between kebabs to make them less sticky. You can either put them on kebab skewers, or just form them into a long sausage shape and place them on the baking sheet. (The authentic way to form them is to make them much thinner and longer than the ones you see here. I do them like this because it's much easier, logistically.) If you have more than you need, or are cooking ahead, you can put them on an extra baking sheet to flash freeze.

Cook them under the broiler under full heat. This will be very quick, about 5 minutes on each side. You'll know they're done when they start to brown a bit and smell ridiculously good. For the ones that you have frozen, bake straight from the freezer at 450° F (230° C) for 8-10 minutes on each side.

Garnish the Chelo Kebabs with fresh herbs and lemon wedges, and serve with cucumber yogurt salad and rice (we do Cauliflower Rice, page 33).

# Cucumber Yogurt Salad

This is a really simple, adaptable salad that's light and refreshing. If you've enjoyed *tatziki* before, then you'll love this.

## Ingredients

1 cup Greek-style yogurt

1/2 teaspoon salt

freshly ground pepper

1/4 cup fresh chopped herbs– one or any combination of the following: dill, mint, coriander (cilantro) parsley or oregano

1 tablespoon extra-virgin olive oil

1 tablespoon fresh lemon juice

half of an English cucumber, chopped into fine dice

## Instructions

Combine everything except for the cucumbers into a bowl, and whisk together until the olive oil is fully incorporated. Taste and see if this dressing needs more salt or lemon juice.

Stir in the diced cucumber and garnish with fresh herbs, and drizzle with a little olive oil.

Enjoy! We eat this as a salad itself, or as a dip or condiment.

# Traveling (And Cooking) To Connect

One of the reasons my family loves to travel is to connect with other people. Although I am pretty shy, I love and enjoy people, and believe that one of the biggest purposes of life is to connect with other humans. We share so much, and real connection is life-giving. That's one reason why we sometimes try to stay with strangers. Although our world is coming together globally through the internet and easy travel options, I think we're also somehow becoming more and more isolated, as we are more dependent on technology and less so on other humans. I think we're losing something big.   I want to share about our recent experience with "couchsurfing," and why the small risk of accepting kindness from strangers is incredibly rewarding.

We somewhat randomly booked a trip to Trieste, Italy when Jeff found out that he had a few days off of work coming up. Airfares were great, and we wanted to go south after a very long winter. We had the option of booking a cheap hotel, but decided to look for hosts on couchsurfing.org instead. I was contacted by Anika, inviting us to come stay with them for the five nights we needed. She said that she and her husband Antonio don't speak much English, but could hopefully get by, and that their son Marco who is Amelia's age didn't speak any. (Children who don't speak the same language are not a real concern, in my experience– they always manage to transcend language.) We said yes, and began exchanging brief emails about details. She said they were kind of busy and unable to take us to see their area. I was just thankful to have a place to stay, and for the opportunity to meet their family.

Our expectation was that we would mostly just sleep at their home, and buy some groceries and cook food for our family in their kitchen. Maybe we would take them out to dinner, or share a meal or two with them, but I didn't want to be any kind of inconvenience to them. Anika offered to pick us up in Trieste after we took the shuttle from the airport, which we really appreciated. There's a bus stop half a kilometer from their home, so we planned to find our way around via public transportation after that. Again, all I wanted was to be as little trouble for their family as possible– we would be their first couchsurfers, and I wanted them to have a good experience and not feel like they had to do much for us.

Well, that last part didn't quite go as planned. This trip was full of mishaps. Although these things are normal, they feel much worse when they affect other people– at least, in my mind! From Jeff having his iphone stolen as soon as we arrived, to tearing one of their window shades (it was easily repaired, but I was mortified). I was feeling unwell for most of the trip, and that added extra stress. Plus, one afternoon I ate something I was allergic to, and got sick. The weather for the first few days was truly terrible, and we had not packed the right clothes and got soaked and frozen on our day in Trieste, which was pretty miserable. Then I had issues with charging my phone, and we were out of communication at times. A bus we took back to their house dropped us off too early, and we were wandering around the hills with a dead cell phone for a while looking for their house (we got there, we were fine!). On the morning of our last day, someone stepped heavily on me, and broke a bone in my foot.

So, lots of these kinds of things happened… Making us feel kind of lame, and embarrassed that we perhaps seemed disorganized, clumsy and needy. That was the opposite of the impression I had hoped to make. And this is where tremendous grace came in. Our hosts were wonderful, and did not treat us like anything but valued guests. The room they put us in was really nice, with a view over the bay and our own bathroom. They wanted to feed us, wanted to take care of anything they could for us. They didn't understand my resistance to grabbing breakfast from their refrigerator or my hesitancy to tell them we hadn't eaten dinner yet (there were no restaurants we could walk to, which was part of our plan). We ended up eating every dinner with them. Anika wouldn't let me clear dishes or load the dishwasher. Antonio opened many, many bottles of great wine for us over those six days, and enthusiastically explained as much about them as he could in his limited English. He pulled out bottles of wine, olive oil, liqueurs and olives that were made by his friends– the very best items in one's pantry, in my opinion.

On the second evening, they invited friends over who speak more English. This family spent the night, and we spent a long evening at the table talking about Slovenian history and cultural differences, drinking wine and listening to the kids shrieking happily as they played together.

**I will not say that we all felt like good friends from the moment we met. While that does happen sometimes, it's not realistic. What did happen is that we got to know each other a little awkwardly at first, and there were some cultural things that were tricky. But we kept spending time together and communicated as much as we could until everyone was more comfortable. And we kept eating together.** I quickly learned that Anika is very honest and down-to-earth. Whenever I apologized for something (there was a long list!) she made steady eye contact and made sure I understood that it was *all* totally OK. By the end of our time there, I believed it.

**By Monday, we were friends.** I had earned dish-clearing privileges, and offered to cook dinner for everyone that evening. I asked Antonio to make a fire for me in his outdoor kitchen (dubbed the *laboratorio*) so I could grill vegetables and Chelo Kebabs (page 79), which are very similar to *chivapchichi*, a super-popular sausage in Trieste, which we had eaten almost constantly since we arrived. We had a sweet time at the table with them, and Jeff and I insisted that they not lift a finger to clean up after dinner. They sat in the kitchen and chatted with us while we cleaned, and we stayed up late talking about parenting and good movies.

Antonio insisted that he should take us to the airport the next evening, and we accepted– feeling really thankful instead of needy. The kids hugged tightly, already missing each other when they said goodnight. Amelia and Marco had been friends from the minute they had met each other, and it was so sweet to watch them together all week. We were exhausted when we left– the trip had been harder than usual. But each of us left with such full hearts. We had seen and learned more than we had thought we would. **We had really connected with this family, even more than I had hoped. It really blows my mind that this is possible in a world that often just feels so disconnected.**

I strongly believe that most humans have plenty in common to make a friendship with. But not everyone is willing or able. We met a couple that loves people, and was willing to take the risk of having us in their home for a week. We took a similar leap of faith, and it was so rewarding. They showed us so much grace and kindness, and we hope we brought something sweet into their lives, as well. It was a joy to be cooked for, and to be able to make food for them in return. There is a very special kind of communion that happens at the table.

Growing up, my family always welcomed newcomers into our home, and it felt normal and right. I have learned that this isn't necessarily common, and so it's something I intentionally want to share with Amelia– to trust people and to assume that we have enough in common to make a meaningful connection. **It can be somewhat counter-cultural, but I think it's important to choose to trust rather than to fear the people around us.** We must do this sensibly, of course, but there are so many wonderful people out there to meet, and we have a lot to offer one another– not the least of which is good food.

# Za'atar Chicken

I'm not sure why, but I have cooked somewhat differently everywhere we have lived. The foods we cooked in one place faded into the background as I started making meals in my new home and country. We used to eat a whole lot of venison roasts in Germany, for example, and our Portland weekly staple-- Za'atar Chicken-- was all but forgotten for a few years after our move. But this is one dish that we have brought back into our lives, because for us, it is the ultimate comfort food. I can't say why this is, exactly-- I never ate these flavors growing up, I've never been to any Middle Eastern countries besides Turkey (which was years after I started eating this dish). But it makes us feel at home every time.

One day, when I was shopping at a little Middle Eastern Market, perusing the bulk spices, I saw something I hadn't tried before. I scooped up an ounce of this green, fragrant spice blend, and decided to learn how to use it. Za'atar is a combination of wild thyme, oregano, marjoram, sesame seeds, and sumac. There are of course a number of variations, many including additional spices. All different types that I've tried have been wonderful.

 Trying this new spice blend lead to the creation of one of our very favorite meals ever-- full of pleasantly stimulating herbal flavors, the pungency of whole lemons, and the comfort of plenty of buttery chicken. I later discovered that this meal is also successfully made with beef-- if that's what you have on hand-- and is great as a crock pot meal.

This meal is wonderful over rice or Cauliflower Rice (page 33). I like to serve it with olives, Tahini Sauce (page 59), homemade Sauerkraut (page 160) or Pickled & Perfumed Pink Onions (page 71) plus a green salad on the side.
(Serves 6)

Ingredients

1/3 cup of butter

two medium-sized yellow onions

6 boneless chicken pieces– can be white or dark– I prefer thighs
(note: I have used bone-in chicken as well, but if you do, be sure to go through and pull out the bones before serving)

two organic lemons, washed, and one of them quartered and thinly sliced, seeds removed

2 cups chicken stock or water

3 tablespoons za'atar spice blend*

salt and pepper to taste

veggies-- turnips or zucchini (optional)

1/2 cup chopped fresh parsley or cilantro

* To make your own za'atar spice blend, combine 4 teaspoons toasted sesame seeds, 4 tablespoons thyme, 2 teaspoons dried marjoram, 2 teaspoons dried oregano, 4 teaspoons ground sumac, and 1 teaspoon sea salt in a blender and process until finely mixed. Store in a jar in the fridge for up to a week.

Ingredients

Put about a tablespoon of the butter into a 5 quart dutch oven.

Chop the onions into wedges, and sauté in the butter.

Add the chicken pieces to the pot, and then add the sliced lemon, and squeeze in the juice of half of the other lemon. Add the chicken stock, za'atar spice blend, the remaining butter, and salt and pepper to taste.

Turn the heat up to high, until everything is boiling. Then turn the heat down low, and let simmer for at least half an hour, and up to two hours. You can also move the simmering pot to a 350° F (180° C) oven for long, slow cooking (2- 3 hours).

About 20 minutes before the end of the cooking time, add the optional veggies, and continue to cook until soft. (If there is still a lot of liquid in the pot, take the lid off for the remainder of the cooking time).

The meat should now be really tender and shred easily with two forks. Remove from heat. Taste it, and add more lemon juice or salt as needed. Throw in the fresh parsley or cilantro, and give it a quick stir.

# Garlic & Herb Greek Lamb Kebabs

Confession: I have cooked lamb a few times and then been totally unable to eat it. Sometimes lamb is just way too... Lamb-y. There are a couple of ways to tame the "gamey" flavor of lamb. One is to buy only very lean cuts. The other is to bring in some serious flavor that can stand up to it and complement those notes. A little time in a good marinade helps even more.

Garlic, lemon and herbs go a long way toward making the most of a good piece of lamb. We love this recipe for Greek Lamb Kebabs, and I think you will, too. It's super simple and quick to make. We even took some of this camping a couple of summers ago, and cooked it on the beach on a little disposable grill– one of our best meals ever. I love making this recipe in the summertime. These flavors are so perfect in the warmer weather, and things like eggplant, tomatoes, peppers and other things that go so well together are all in season. Leftover Greek Lamb Kebabs are fantastic chopped and added to herbal green salads for lunch or dinner the next day. (Serves 6)

## Ingredients

2 cups fresh herbs– any combination of parsley, cilantro, fresh mint, or oregano, and do try to use some fresh thyme

5 cloves fresh garlic (more if your cloves are very small)

1 tablespoon sea salt

1/4 cup olive oil

juice of one lemon

1 teaspoon whole cumin seed

cayenne pepper or chili flakes, optional

2 lbs. (1 kilo) of lamb shoulder cut into 1 inch cubes

in terms of equipment, you'll need a food chopper or blender. In a pinch you can use a mortar and pestle but it will be more work and not come out creamy– but still worth it! You will also need some shish kebab skewers.

## Instructions

Make the marinade. Put everything but the lamb into your food chopper and blend until smooth.

Put your lamb in a glass container and coat with the marinade. Use your hands to turn the meat so it all gets coated. Let sit for at least an hour, but overnight is even better.

Slide the pieces of meat onto some shish kebab skewers.

Grill them over the barbecue, or broil them– which is what we usually do. I put the skewers across a small baking tray so they don't drip all over the oven, and broil on full for about 7 minutes on each side.

Serve with Tahini Sauce (page 59), feta, olives, rice (we love Cauliflower Rice, page 33) and a green salad.

This marinade is also good on chicken and beef. I usually make a double-batch and store half in a glass jar in the fridge. It will last for at least a couple of weeks, and makes the prep work for another dinner so quick.

# Mercadillo Agricultur: Visiting an Open Market in Tenerife

My very favorite thing to do as a tourist is to shop for food. Usually the first stop I make in a new place is at the supermarket, where I take my time strolling down each of the aisles, noticing all that is interesting and different from other grocery stores. Next, I find out when the next open market will be held, and where. Shopping at open markets is one of my very favorite things in the world to do. As I have mentioned before, shopping at open markets is a formative experience from my childhood in the Philippines, which I have always tried to continue no matter where I have lived.

So when we arrived in Tenerife, the first order of business after settling in to our place in Icod de los Vinos was to locate a supermarket and then find out about the open market. Luck would have it that it was happening the next morning, a 15 minute drive from us, in La Guancha.

There were lots of people there, and although plenty looked like either foreigners or tourists, it was clear that a stop at the market after church on a Sunday was just standard routine for many local families. Lots of people were standing around chatting and eating, and the environment was relaxed and warm.

All the vendors seemed to love Amelia, and she had her cheeks pinched and hair caressed and was handed as much fruit as she could eat. Even Jeff and I were given bananas, and no one was pushy about us buying anything, but we were offered plenty of samples. I **loved** seeing a blend of produce– things I ate in the Philippines as a kid, produce that grows beautifully in Southern California where I'm from, plus root veggies and brassicas that are ubiquitous here and in other cooler climates. All of it grows locally in Tenerife!

There were lots of herb stands– for culinary use, medicinal purposes (including packets of dried stevia leaves) and for planting in the garden. Fresh herbs and citrus are ingredients I pine for daily. I can buy them here in the UK, but of course none of the citrus is ever local and has made an exhausting journey by the time it reaches me. And the fresh herbs lack the vigor of having grown in the sunshine, for most of the year at least. So, I was in heaven.

We brought home loads of fruit, vegetables, and herbs. We also picked up a hard local cheese (I can't remember the name, but it was sheep's milk and very much like a caramel-flavored parmesan) and some seriously delicious local sausages.

To be honest, we left before I felt truly ready to go– which always seems to be the case. But I had walked by each stall four times, and was beginning to feel kind of conspicuous!

We ate extremely well all week, cooking most of our meals at home and tasting flavors I had been missing for what felt like a lifetime of living in northern climates. The meal we made first when we returned from the Mercadillo Agricultur was the recipe that follows, Spring to Life Chicken (page 90).

It was wonderful to enjoy such fresh, sunny flavors straight from the market.

# Spring to Life Grilled Chicken

When we visited Tenerife for the first time, one of our greatest pleasures was cooking and eating fresh food that we bought at the local open market. I especially loved all of the citrus and fresh herbs that were available, along with summer crops like red peppers and eggplant! Here is a meal that we really loved– it was simple to prepare, and I was able to make it without any kitchen gadgets– just a mortar and pestle. By the way, my daughter named this dish– "Spring to Life"– which is how she felt about the zesty lemon and the wonderful herbs! I think you'll love this recipe because it's so simple and fresh. We really enjoyed the leftovers the next day, too. (Serves 6)

## Ingredients

1 1/2 cups fresh herbs– can be any combination of parsley, cilantro, fresh mint, or oregano

4 cloves fresh garlic (more if your cloves are very small)

2 tablespoons coarse sea salt

1/4 cup olive oil

juice of one lemon

cayenne pepper or chili flakes, optional

6 chicken legs, skin-on
(Of course, you can also use a whole chicken broken into parts, or whatever you like. But the legs are the most flavorful.)

You'll need a mortar and pestle or a little food chopper or blender. An immersion blender would also work well.

## Instructions

Roughly chop the herbs, and put them into the mortar bowl. Add the garlic cloves and salt, and mash them well. Sideways movements will help turn them into a paste.

Add the lemon juice and olive oil, and incorporate them, making a marinade. Add the chili or cayenne, if using.

Coat the chicken pieces with the marinade, and leave for several hours– overnight is best. I usually like to do this in a ziplock bag.

Grill the chicken, or broil in your oven, until golden and crispy, juices running clear when pricked.

We like to eat ours with grilled peppers and eggplant slices. I sometimes also make a fresh herb salad to go with– chopping the same type of herbs I used for my marinade and tossing them with lemon juice, olive oil and a little salt– it's the perfect, bright compliment to the marinated chicken– these flavors certainly do spring to life!

# Thai Grilled Chicken
# with Lemongrass, Basil & Lime

Which sorts of flavors do you crave when it's hot out? For me, it's a tie between Central American and Southeast Asian. I invented this recipe when I had an intense craving for some pungent Asian flavors, but I wanted something light– not like curry, but more reminiscent of the barbecued street food you might find in Asia. I happened to have a good collection of bright, aromatic herbs on hand, so Thai Grilled Chicken with Lemongrass, Basil & Lime was just perfect for these hankerings. (Serves 6)

## Ingredients

1 stalk of fresh lemongrass, cut into smaller pieces

4 cloves garlic

the juice of 1 or 2 limes (some of them can be pretty dry)

a one inch piece of ginger, peeled and roughly chopped

about 1/4 cup (packed) of fresh basil, roughly chopped

one small, seeded chile– optional if you like it spicy

1 teaspoons fish sauce, optional

2 teaspoons sea salt

1/4 cup of avocado oil (this oil has the highest smoke point of all plant-based oils, and so is most stable for grilling)

one whole chicken, cut into pieces, or six bone-in, skin-on chicken pieces

## Instructions

Make the marinade: Put all ingredients into a small food processor and blend until everything is chopped fine and blended like a salad dressing. You can also use an immersion blender, if you have the cylindrical part to use it in.

Put the chicken in a glass container and coat evenly with the marinade. Let it sit in the fridge for at least an hour, and overnight is even better.

You have a couple options for cooking. This is great on the grill. But in case you don't feel like firing up the grill, I usually use a broiler pan under the broiler on its highest setting.

Cook skin-side down first, and be sure to brush on any leftover marinade. I don't usually set a timer, but prefer to gauge by the chicken's color– I wait till it's golden, and browning slightly, then flip the pieces. It's done when the skin is golden and bubbly. If you prefer to go with time, then about 20 minutes on each side is a good bet.

Remove from the heat and let rest for a few minutes before serving.

This dish is great with a cabbage slaw and grilled veggies. We make two chickens like this at a time so we can enjoy it in Asian-inspired salads and lettuce wraps.

# Carne Asada

This is the perfect summer grilling food, and I just couldn't get enough of it during my pregnancy. If we were to go strictly based on raw materials used, then when my daughter Amelia was born I'd say she was made of about 50% Carne Asada. Maybe I was making up for the previous five years of being meatless. Or maybe it's just because it is so darned delicious. For years since, one of my favorite meals of all time has been Carne Asada, and Chocolate Black Beans (page 46), served with Roasted Tomatillo Salsa (page 65), guacamole and Sangria (page 133). This meal *always* feels like a party. (Serves 6)

Ingredients

2 lbs flank steak

3 garlic cloves, peeled

1/3 cup packed fresh cilantro leaves

1/4 cup fresh lime juice

1/4 cup fresh orange juice

1/4 cup avocado oil (you can melt bacon fat instead, and it's fantastic)

2 teaspoons ground cumin

1/4 teaspoon ground chipotle or cayenne pepper (optional)

1 teaspoon sea salt

freshly ground black pepper

extra cilantro for garnish

Instructions

Make the marinade. Put all of the ingredients except for the steak in a food processor or blender, and blend until smooth. You could also leave out the cilantro until the end, and just blend briefly to keep some of the texture of the leaves.

Marinate the beef. You can use a zip-lock bag and press all of the air out after you add the meat and the marinade. Or you can put it in a shallow glass dish and coat both sides and cover, turning the meat over once halfway through. Let the meat marinate for *at least* an hour, and up to overnight.

Grill the meat. Over a wood or charcoal fire is best. However, I have also had success with doing it under the broiler in a broiler pan on the highest heat.

You want to cook this hot and fast, searing both sides and flipping over a couple of times. Medium-rare is ideal in my opinion (about four minutes each side) and you don't want to go to well-done, as the meat will get a bit tough.

Let the meat rest for ten minutes, then slice thinly across the grain.

Garnish with the fresh cilantro.

# Easy Moroccan–Spiced Beef
## with Lemons & Butternut Squash

When I came up with this recipe, it was in the middle of winter. The sun was so low in the sky, and it had already been dark for two hours or more by the time we sat down to eat dinner.

I don't have a lot of time to spend in the kitchen, but I love to have something in the oven, making the house smell so good and comforting at the end of the day. This recipe for Moroccan Beef Stew is something I've been making regularly. It's one of those "cheater" kinds of stews requiring no browning of meat or any kind of cooking diligence. I put it all in the pot, let it cook in the oven, then add some vibrant chunks of butternut squash at the end– for a meal that is bright, warming, and seems like something that took a whole lot more effort than it really did. The *ras el hanout* is floral and warming, and cooking lemons with their peels produces a flavor that is vivid, pungent and slightly sweet. Just what we need on a cold wintry evening!

## Ingredients

3 medium yellow onions, roughly chopped

2 lbs. (or 1 kilo) beef cut into 1 inch chunks

2 tablespoons ras el hanout spice blend

1 tablespoon sea salt

1 teaspoon freshly ground black pepper

1/3 cup unsalted butter

3 cloves garlic, crushed

2 cups beef stock

2 organic lemons (1 of them quartered and thinly sliced, seeds removed)

1 medium butternut squash, peeled and seeded, cut into 1 inch chunks

1 bunch fresh cilantro, roughly chopped

1 cup of leafy greens, chopped (optional)

you will also need a dutch oven or similar pot that can be put in the oven

## Instructions

Place all of the ingredients except for the butternut and cilantro into your dutch oven.

Bring to a simmer on your stovetop over medium-high heat, then move to a 300° F (150° C ) oven and cook for 2 hours.

Add the butternut squash and stir into the pot, scraping the bottom with a wooden spoon. If you are using some greens, then now is the time to add the chopped stems. If the stew is already thick, you can add some more liquid.

Cook in the oven for 1/2 an hour more, until the squash is tender.

Take your stew out of the oven. Stir it up and taste it. If needed, add extra lemon juice and salt. Stir in the leafy greens, if using. Throw the chopped cilantro in the pot and cover again for a few minutes, until the herbs turn bright green.

Serve over rice (we eat ours with Cauliflower Rice, page 33) or eat it on its own as you would a hearty stew. Enjoy!

* Note: This recipe can also be made in a crockpot, following instructions for your favorite crockpot stew and adding the cilantro at the end.

# Coconut Chicken Curry

When we need a meal that is warm and comforting, I make Coconut Chicken Curry. It's easy to cook, and incredibly good. Keep in mind that you can substitute most of the vegetables for whatever you have on hand to make this curry– I would just stay away from things like celery, parsnips, and celeriac in this one.

I often serve ours on top of blanched cabbage ribbons, but it's also great over rice (we like Cauliflower Rice, page 33) or zucchini noodles. This is always a big hit over here, makes great leftovers, and can be made in larger batches. (Serves 6)

## Ingredients

2 tablespoons coconut oil

1 whole chicken, cut into parts (I kept the wings out, to use them for chicken stock)

3 onions, yellow or white

3-4 carrots

1 turnip

1 inch piece of ginger, smashed

3 cloves garlic, smashed

2 tablespoons curry powder

1 teaspoon fenugreek seeds

fresh ground pepper

salt

one 14 oz (400 mL) can coconut milk (not low fat, please!)

lemon juice, lime juice, or apple cider vinegar

a small bunch of cilantro

## Instructions

In a large pot, heat up your coconut oil over medium heat. Put the chicken pieces in, skin-side-down, to brown. You will probably need to do this in a couple batches. Give them plenty of time– if you try to turn them too soon, the skin will stick to the bottom. If they release easily, then they are probably ready to turn. Brown the other side, too. Remove the pieces from the pot when they're browned.

Add your onions to the oil in the pan, and use a wooden spatula to scrape up the bits of chicken stuck to the bottom of the pan. Let them cook for about 4 minutes or so, then add the carrots and keep scraping for another minute or two. Salt a little as you go, to build flavor.

Add the spices, ginger and garlic in, and stir them with the vegetables and let them toast in the oil for about a minute– you don't want them to burn, just to get really fragrant.

Add the turnips, put the chicken pieces back into the pot, and pour in the coconut milk. Add a little hot water to the can to rinse and add that to the pot, as well– the liquid should be about to the chicken on top.

Cover and cook for 45 minutes to an hour.

Check for seasoning*, and add lemon juice to taste– a nice little acid kick here is important for flavor balance. Add more salt or pepper, if needed. Top with chopped cilantro right before serving.

*Here's an extra tip for cooking with Indian spices: If you don't think your dish is flavorful enough at the end of cooking, you can add a wonderful, pungent kick of flavor by heating up some oil and toasting more spices and garlic in the hot oil to add to the pot right before you serve. This is especially great for dishes like lentils, that can get bland as they cook for a long time.

# A Delicious Day in Brugges

I had heard some mixed reviews of Brugges. On the one hand, people said it was really sweet and cute, very idyllic. However, others said that this had been taken to an extreme, and that it was just a big tourist trap. So I wasn't *that* excited to go, but felt like I should check it off my list. I'm glad we went.

It's a wonderful little city, even though it *is* full of tourists. I totally get why they are all there– Brugges is great!
We parked in a huge underground parking garage, which turned out to be super-cheap! When we got out of the car, even a couple levels below ground, we smelled really good food– the air was thick with waffles and fries!

I was super excited to see that we had made it to Brugges during a weekly open market. It reminded me so much of our local market when we lived in Germany– not quite so much fresh produce, but lots of prepared meats, cheeses and other foodie delights.
There were a surprising number of roasted meat vendors. It all looked (and smelled!) really incredible, and the lines were very long! One of my favorite sights was locals packing bags of their purchases into their bike baskets– what a fun way to shop! *So* many cheese carts… Fresh, local, hand-paddled butter! All sorts of things we love…

Here's the sad part– we walked around, and I just focused on taking pictures. We figured we'd come back around lunch time and buy some of that delicious rotisserie meat, olives, cheese, etc. for an incredible picnic lunch, later. Alas, we should have asked what time the market ended– we found it had closed already when we were starving and we came back to buy ourselves some lunch…. Next time!

We enjoyed walking all over the city and seeing all of the beautiful architecture. Brugges really is a gorgeous city, and everyone seemed to be having a wonderful time.

We ended our time in Brugges with a meal in the market square. What an incredible feeling, to be surrounded by such gorgeous architecture, with people from all over the world enjoying some sunshine and Belgian beer.

Jeff had a beer called Kwak, which is named after the sound it makes sloshing back into its bulbous glass. Funny, right? One more little bit of trivia– these wooden-handled steins were so popular at one point that customers had to turn in one shoe as a deposit when they ordered Kwak, to ensure that they did not leave with the glass it came in! I should have taken a pictures of the larger beer sizes– they were like this one, but about as tall as your knee!

We loved our day in Brugges, and can't wait to go back again!

# Wintry Oxtail Glazed With Red Wine, Orange & Rosemary

The first time I tried oxtail, it was right after we moved to England– I found a compelling recipe in a Nigel Slater cookbook I had just bought my husband, and we found some oxtail at a local farm shop. My experience eating them was very similar to the first time I cooked and ate beef ribs: I was overcome with intense regret over the many years that I didn't eat meat and missed this dish! Braised oxtail is sticky, sweet, dark and addictive. It became an instant family favorite, and I admit that we are all a little greedy about those bony little knobs of meat-candy.

I like to serve ours with an herbal green salad, Celeriac Puree (page 38) and homemade Sauerkraut (page 160). I always save the remains for brewing an extra-rich beef stock (page 158).

(Serves three, but it's very likely you'll feel you haven't had enough!)

## Ingredients

an oxtail, cut into joints

2 tablespoons butter, bacon grease or beef tallow

2 onions

3 carrots

several cloves of garlic

2 bay leaves

a whole orange– cut in half, with one of the halves cut into wedges

a couple sprigs of rosemary

salt and pepper

1/2 a bottle of an assertive red wine (I used Rioja)

## Instructions

Set the oven to 325° F (160° C). On the stove top, heat up the fat in a dutch oven.

Brown your meat, rendering (cooking down) some of the fat on the oxtail pieces, and using tongs to turn it and get as much surface as you can. Remove to a plate. Use all the fat and crispy bits in your pan to brown the onion and carrots, scraping with a wooden spatula. Squeeze half of the orange and keep scraping to deglaze the pan. Season with salt and pepper.

Add the meat back in, and add the garlic, rosemary, bay leaves, and orange wedges, and season again. Pour in the wine, and bring it all to a boil over high heat.

Cover the pot or skillet well, and put it in the oven. Let it braise slowly there, turning the meat after one hour, and checking to make sure there's still liquid in the pan. Return to the oven for another hour, for a total of two hours braising time. The liquid should reduce almost completely, leaving the meat coated in a warm, sticky glaze. Enjoy!

# Woodland Venison Stew

This stew was inspired by a magical day in the woods here in England, finding edible purple mushrooms in a birch forest, walking through fern-covered woodlands, and listening to foxes barking. I love the idea of cooking proteins with the foods in their natural environment. In this case, mushrooms, juniper berries, and thyme seemed especially appropriate companions for the venison.

It's nourishing and delicious! I like the simplicity of this stew– there aren't too many components, and the basic, woodsy flavors of mushrooms, juniper and thyme come through really nicely. (Serves 6)

## Ingredients

1 tablespoon beef tallow or ghee

2 pounds (1 kilo) venison, cubed

3 chopped yellow or white onions (mine were pretty small, so I used 4)

3 medium carrots, cut into 1/4-inch slices, or baby carrots, peeled

1 1/2 cups cleaned and quartered mushrooms

3 cloves garlic, smashed

a few sprigs of fresh thyme

1 tablespoon juniper berries (give them a quick smash with a mortar and pestle, if possible)

salt to taste

black pepper to taste

2 cups beef, lamb, or venison stock, or dry red wine

1/4 cup red wine vinegar or apple cider vinegar

Please feel free to substitute what you have available, as always. I think parsnips or celeriac would go nicely here, for example.

## Instructions

Start by browning your venison. Heat up some fat in your pan over moderate heat, and give the venison plenty of time to brown. Once it's nicely seared on at least two sides, pull it out and let it rest.

Add the onions and scrape up the crispy bits from the bottom of the pan with a wooden spatula. After about 5 minutes of cooking and scraping, add the carrots and mushrooms, and do it some more, until they look like they have picked up a little color.

Add the garlic, juniper berries, thyme, and salt and pepper, and let them get some of that high heat in the pan, before adding the liquid.
Add the liquid and quickly give the pan a few scrapes to clean up any caramelized vegetable bits, and mix them into the pot. Add the meat, and make sure you have enough liquid to cover. Add more salt and pepper. Cover the pot and reduce the heat to low-medium, and let it simmer for a couple of hours. About half way through the cooking, add the vinegar. I used apple cider vinegar, since it's apple season, and that seemed like a good match for the forest flavors.

When everything is tender, and the liquid has reduced into a nice sauce, taste and see if you need to add any more salt, pepper, or vinegar before serving. A little fresh thyme wouldn't hurt, either! I like to serve this with Root Veggie Puree (page 162).

# Deeply-Rooted Beef Stew

After a few months of lighter summertime meals, I am ready to put something on the stove and leave it all afternoon, filling the house with that cozy, nurturing smell of a hearty meal. This is all part of my coping plan for making peace with long winter seasons, and I do welcome the colder months for the sake of such rich meals, as much as for the opportunity to slow down.

One of my favorite elements of cold-weather eating is root vegetables– so sweet, earthy and satisfying, especially when they are given ample time to soften in meaty juices. I like to serve this meal with a creamy Cauliflower Puree (page 162) and some homemade Sauerkraut (page 160).
(Serves 6)

Ingredients

1 kilo or 2 lbs. shin of beef or other good stew meat

Bacon grease, beef tallow, or butter

3 onions, sliced

3 carrots, peeled and cut into chunky slices

2 parsnips, peeled and cut into chunky slices

3 cups (750mL) beef stock, red wine, or dry cider

3 cloves garlic, crushed

3 bay leaves

1 teaspoon coriander seeds

a few juniper berries

1/2 teaspoon fenugreek seeds

1/4 cup red wine vinegar

3 sprigs of thyme

Other veggies you have on hand, optional.

Instructions

Start by heating up some fat to brown your meat in. I like to use bacon grease or beef tallow. Put your meat in, fattiest side down (to render some extra fat) and don't crowd it too much. You'll want to keep things nice and hot, so that the meat browns rather than steams. Take your time with this part of the process, as it is one of the best ways to build great, rich flavor into your stew. Turn and brown at least the other side of the meat, and all sides if you have the time. I had to do this in a couple of batches.

While you're waiting for the meat to brown is the perfect time to start chopping vegetables, so it doesn't end up being too time-consuming. By the time you're ready to pull all of your meat out and set it aside, you should have a nice pile of onions cut into wedges (hopefully some carrots and parsnips, too, but you still have time to do that while the onions cook, anyway).

Cook those onions, scraping up the brown bits from the bottom of the pan– for about five minutes. Add the carrots and parsnips, and cook the same way for a few more minutes. Add your spices: garlic, bay leaves, juniper berries, fenugreek and some pepper and salt.

Give the seeds and garlic a minute to get aromatic, and then add the beef stock (or wine). Give it a good, firm stirring, to get any remaining sticky stuff off the bottom of the pan, and then add the browned beef back in.

Add more liquid if you need to, so that the meat is mostly covered. Add more salt and pepper. Put the lid on and and turn the heat down to low. Let this simmer for at least an hour. I try to let it go for three, since the longer cooking breaks down all of the sinew and cartilage in the meat into a really velvety sauce and incredibly tender meat. (If you have less time, cut the meat into smaller pieces, and that should help speed things along.)

About halfway through the cooking time, I add vinegar– for red meat, I usually use red wine vinegar, but apple cider vinegar is good, too. (If you used red wine for your liquid, you won't need as much.) The vinegar not only gives it a nice acidic flavor balance, but it helps to break down the collagen in the meat.

When everything is looking and smelling like it's about ready, you have the option of adding some quick-cooking vegetables, to add a little extra brightness and texture (and stretch the stew!). I usually like to add some kale. (Greens cook very quickly, so I save those for the last couple minutes. The flimsier greens, I add after I turn the heat off, and just let them steam.) Regardless of whether you add more veg, put in your thyme at the end, so the flavors will stay bright.

Always taste before bringing it to the table. I often end up adding a little more acid and salt. Usually, the liquid has reduced to a nice, thick sauce– even without any flour or starch. If it's too watery, take out the meat and veggies, and cook it down at high heat for a few minutes, and stir some butter in at the end. (But that probably won't be necessary!)

Tip: Don't wait until the end of your cooking to season with salt and pepper– do that throughout your cooking, and it will build depth of flavor.

Sweets

I believe in desserts. They are one of the simplest pleasures, and are a wonderful way to celebrate and enjoy life. The way my family eats would certainly be described by most as "healthy," but I would rather we just talk about eating joyfully and enjoying our food. We eat desserts regularly– but don't go for just any old sugary bite. I like to make sure we're getting the really good stuff. Home-made, with quality ingredients. Good chocolate, rich butter, real vanilla, and using more natural sweeteners when possible, for a fuller flavor.

I'll confess that one reason this is important to me is that I hope that my daughter will learn to distinguish between junk foods and quality sweets and treats- that the cheap stuff will just not taste quite right, after enjoying so many wonderful desserts at home and on our travels.

The following recipes are some that we make at home over and over again. In fact, my husband is setting a slice of Chocolate Espresso Cake next to me as I am typing. **This is a cookbook fueled by chocolate, espresso and love.**

# Carrot & Parsnip Cake
## with Lemon Cream Cheese Frosting

Confession: I am not really one to get super-excited about cake. Cakes are very pretty, but I tend to crave more savory morsels, and dense, rich desserts. So, last fall, I was surprised to find that I'd been suddenly thinking a lot about cake. I kept recalling in my mind all of the signs in restaurant windows in Germany alerting one to the availability of *Kaffee und Kuchen* (coffee and cake). As it had gotten chilly and gray over here, *Kaffee und Kuchen* sounded just amazing. And in particular, coffee and Carrot Cake had been calling my name for weeks.

I usually nurse a craving for weeks before I attempt to satisfy it. (I know!! I need to stop that!) Then, after I have built it up so long that whatever it is I've been imagining myself eating is incredible, I usually feel bitter disappointment as soon as I take a bite. I remember one time going to a doughnut shop, buying an apple fritter, taking a bite and then dropping it into the trash can. Nothing can live up to the fantasy of my long-held cravings. Well, *almost* nothing. I want to share a cake that went above and beyond to deliver the bliss I had imagined– but, skeptically, not fully expected. Carrot and Parsnip Cake is where it's at for me when a sweet, cake-y craving hits.

# Carrot & Parsnip Cake

## Ingredients

3 cups finely ground almond flour

1 teaspoon baking soda

1 teaspoon sea salt

1 tablespoon cinnamon

1/2 teaspoon nutmeg

5 eggs

½ cup honey (maple syrup would work, too)

¼ cup coconut oil melted

1 tablespoon grated fresh ginger (or 1 teaspoon dried ginger, optional)

2 cups grated carrots

1 cup grated parsnips

3/4 cup chopped dates

1 cup walnuts, roughly chopped (toasting them in the oven for a few minutes first is highly recommended, but not obligatory)

## Instructions

Combine the first five dry ingredients in a large bowl.

In another, smaller bowl, mix the eggs, honey, oil, and ginger together.

Add the wet ingredients to the dry ones and stir only until combined.

Add the grated vegetables, dates and walnuts to the batter, and fold them in evenly– don't over-mix.

Pour the batter into a greased round 9-inch cake pan.

Bake the cake at 325° F (165° C) for about 55 minutes, or until the edges are brown and a toothpick inserted into the center comes out clean.

Let cool, and make your frosting (if using) and then frost it.

Serve with a good cup of coffee (or tea).

# Lemon Cream Cheese Frosting

## Ingredients

8 ounces (1 cup) cream cheese at room temperature

1 stick (or 8 tablespoons) unsalted butter at room temperature

1/3 cup of honey

1 tablespoon of lemon zest

## Instructions

Put the cream cheese in a medium-sized bowl, and begin working to soften it with a wooden spoon or spatula. Add the butter to it gradually and mix, until they are well combined.

Add the honey and lemon zest and whip with a whisk until blended and light.

Taste and adjust the sweetness and tartness (from lemon juice), and frost your cake.

# Chocolate Espresso Cake

In the darker months of the year, Chocolate Espresso Cake is exactly what I need. In the afternoon, as the sun sets (way too early!) I need a little hit of something– caffeine, pleasure, comfort… Happily, my husband likes to make me chocolate cakes, and he's not afraid to adapt a recipe to suit our family's needs. One of my favorites is Nigel Slater's Chocolate Almond Cake, from <u>The Kitchen Diaries</u> adapted by Jeff to be grain-free. We ate this as part of our Winter Solstice celebrations last year– it's rich and comforting. While there are plenty of flourless chocolate cake recipes out there, I prefer this one because the almond flour gives it a nice crumb and it's much more like a traditional cake– but so dark and decadent.

## Ingredients

7 oz (200g) good quality dark chocolate (not baking chocolate, but eating chocolate!)

a shot of espresso (about 3 tablespoons strong coffee)

1 cup butter, cut into pieces

5 eggs, separated

1 scant cup (200g) sugar– can be regular, or coconut sugar (we often use less, as I like my chocolate more bitter than sweet)

1 teaspoon baking powder

2 tablespoons good quality cocoa powder, plus extra for dusting

200g or 1 3/4 cups almond flour

in terms of equipment, you'll need a double boiler (or a metal bowl atop a pot of water), mixer with a whisk attachment, parchment paper, and a round 9" springform pan

## Instructions

Preheat your oven to 350° F (180° C), and line your pan with buttered parchment paper.

In a double-boiler or a metal bowl set over a pan of simmering water, melt your chocolate. As it begins to soften, add the espresso, stirring gently until completely melted. Add the butter, and stir until everything is even.

Beat the egg whites until stiff, and then fold in the sugar.

Combine the dry ingredients.

Remove the chocolate mixture from the heat, and stir in the egg yolks. Fold the chocolate into the egg whites, gently.

Sift the dry ingredients into the batter, and then stir very gently to combine– do not over-mix. Pour the batter into the cake pan and bake for 50 minutes, until the middle is semi-firm and an inserted knife blade comes out cleanly.

Allow to cool, then dust with cocoa powder and serve.

Don't tell anyone, but I think it's great for breakfast, with a cup of coffee.

# Tahini Molasses Cookies

Ever since we discovered tahini cookies, we have been making and loving our own version of them almost every week. I like them so much that I just have to share them with you. The list of ingredients is so short, and (if I ask him nicely) Jeff can whip up a batch in just a few minutes. They are crispy on the outside with a nice chewiness in the middle.

These tahini molasses cookies are perfect for us because they are grain free and my daughter's school has a "no nuts" policy, and she can take them in her lunches. They aren't too sweet, and I really love the way molasses and tahini work together so well in this cookie. (Makes about a dozen)

## Ingredients

1 cup tahini paste

3/4 cup molasses sugar or dark muscovado sugar

1 teaspoon baking soda

1 large egg

a pinch of sea salt

some sesame seeds for sprinkling the tops of the cookies with

## Instructions

Preheat your oven to 350° F or 180° C.

Combine everything but the sesame seeds in a mixing bowl, stirring the tahini well before measuring. Mix the batter until everything is combined.

Spoon tablespoonfuls onto your cookie sheet, about two inches apart. There can be some variation in the texture of the batter– sometimes it may be more firm than others, but it will always do some spreading while baking, so leave some space for that.

Sprinkle the tops of the cookies with sesame seeds.

Bake for 10-15 minutes, until the edges are a little crispy and it all smells heavenly.

Let them cool for a few minutes before handling, as they will be fragile while they're hot.

Enjoy! I love these with coffee in the morning or tea in the afternoon or evening.

# Saffron & Rose Persian Love Ice Cream

This is an ode to my favorite cake, called Persian Love Cake– it is incredibly light and aromatic. I have made this cake for extra-special occasions, including baby showers, bridal showers, and even my cousin's wedding. One of the best parts of the cake is the saffron and rosewater frosting. This ice cream is a version of that ethereal topping. It is so exotic and wonderful– yet uncomplicated to make!

## Ingredients

2 cups of heavy cream

2 egg yolks

1 small pinch of saffron threads

1/3 cup sugar (honey would also work here)

2 teaspoons rose water

chopped pistachios (totally optional)

dried or fresh rose petals (also totally optional, but pretty!)

An ice cream maker would be ideal, but because of the very high fat content of this recipe, you could also freeze it in a glass container, and scoop it pretty successfully.

## Instructions

Pour half of the cream (put the rest in the fridge or freezer) into a saucepan, and add the saffron threads, sugar and egg yolks.

Turn the heat on low, and gradually warm the cream. Use a whisk to incorporate the egg yolks into the cream and keep things moving, whisking more as the mixture thickens. You are turning the cream into a custard and infusing it with saffron at the same time. You don't want to boil or simmer the cream– just heat it until it thickens.

Once the cream mixture has thickened up a bit, turn off the heat. Add the rose water. Add the cold cream, and stir to incorporate. You are almost done. Taste it to see if you need a little more sweetness (freezing it will dull the sweetness a little, so you should aim for a tad sweeter than you want your ice cream to taste). Also taste that the rosewater is coming through, adding a little more, if needed.

Pour it into your ice cream machine, or into a container to freeze. Give it time to solidify, and then scoop it up!

You can garnish the ice cream with rose petals and/ or chopped pistachios, but it's also just wonderful on its own.

Eat it with someone you love.

# Simple Black Cherry Creme Fraiche Ice Cream

On the way home from the beach one day last summer, we stopped to take a walk along a country foot path. The trip to the beach in Southwold had been a big disappointment– totally cold and windy despite a cheerful forecast– and we wanted to redeem the outing with a peaceful and interesting walk someplace new. I had it in the back of my mind that it was stone fruit season, but didn't really have my hopes up. We had actually gone for a foraging walk the day before, and come back empty-handed.

No matter what the time of year, I'm always looking for something to eat when we're out for a walk. And as you may have guessed, we found something. Cherries. Everywhere. Falling all over the ground, picked at by birds, and ripe, ripe, ripe. We found black cherries and morello cherries, and picked as many as we could carry in our only, already-ripping bag. It turns out that we had over four quarts! Although I wasn't sure what to do with all of them, making this ice cream was the very first thing.

This black cherry ice cream is super simple, and tastes incredibly good. There are only four ingredients, and the creme fraiche adds that extra little tang and buoyant texture that makes it really work. I love how the brown sugar's caramel flavor brings out the dark, raisin-like notes in the super-ripe cherries.

We may not have had a great beach day, but we all ended the day feeling like we were really living the good life– what could be better than an afternoon of picking cherries, and a dessert of fresh-from-the-trees black cherry ice cream? Not much! (Serves 6)

## Ingredients

2 cups pitted black cherries

1 1/3 cups cream or whole milk

1 1/3 cups creme fraiche

1/3 cup brown sugar (honey would also work well here)

an ice cream maker

## Instructions

Combine the cream (or milk,) cherries, and sugar (or honey) in a saucepan. Heat gently until slightly hot (or very warm, whichever works for you!). You don't want to boil it, but you want to coax the juices out of the cherries and dissolve the sugar. Stir and mash the cherries a bit.

Let it cool slightly. Fold in the creme fraiche, and put it in the fridge for an hour– or in the freezer for 20 minutes.

Put it in your ice cream machine, and let it do its thing. Serve up the ice cream and enjoy!

# Vanilla Bean Ice Cream & Affogato Recipe

In the world of food, there are some magical combinations, the sums of which are so much more than the parts they are made of. Affogato is one of these. Friends, I don't know how I went through most of my life without knowing about it, and I consider this post a kind of public service announcement to make sure that it doesn't happen to anyone else. When I had affogato for the first time a few years ago, I was incredulous. How could something so simple be so amazing? This is one of those things I start craving fiendishly on a regular basis. Well, now we make ours at home– and you can, too.

# Vanilla Bean Ice Cream Recipe

Ingredients

2 cups of heavy cream
(You can also use 1 cup of full-fat milk if you want, but then you will definitely need an ice cream maker.)

2 egg yolks

1 vanilla bean, split open

1/3 cup sugar
(You can use evaporated cane juice, and honey is also an option but will definitely change the flavor)

a pinch of sea salt

An ice cream maker would be ideal, but because of the very high fat content of this recipe, you could also freeze it in a glass container, and scoop it pretty successfully.

For the espresso for the affogato, you will need something to generate a shot of espresso with– my favorite is an aeropress, but I think a really strong, short shot from a moka pot could work, if that's what you have.

Instructions

Pour half of the cream into a saucepan, and add the vanilla bean, sugar and egg yolks, and sea salt.

Turn the heat on low, and gradually warm the cream. Use a whisk to incorporate the egg yolks into the cream and keep things moving, whisking more as the mixture thickens. You are turning the cream into a custard and infusing it with vanilla at the same time. You don't want to boil or simmer the cream– just heat it until it thickens.

Once the cream mixture has thickened up a bit, turn off the heat. Add the cold cream, and stir to incorporate. Remove the vanilla bean pod. You are almost done. Taste it to see if you need a little more sweetness. (Freezing it will dull the sweetness a little, so you should aim for a tad sweeter than you want your ice cream to taste.) Chill it to at least room temperature before adding to your ice cream maker.

Pour it into your ice cream maker, or into a container to freeze. Give it time to solidify, and then scoop it up!

Now, to turn this scoop of vanilla ice cream into affogato, you need a shot of espresso. We used to have a little espresso machine that we used for our daily coffee. But we have done away with it, now that we have an aeropress that honestly produces a better shot of espresso than our machine ever did. We are completely hooked, and now making affogato is as easy as heating up a little water and pressing it through some espresso grounds. Pour it on over– err on the side of too little vs. too much espresso, because you don't want to melt all of your ice cream. Enjoy!

The strong flavor of the espresso mingles beautifully with the creamy vanilla, and as it gets colder, forms little ice crystals against the ice cream.

# Two Ingredient Decadent Chocolate Ice Cream

Here is a really easy but blissfully-rich ice cream you can make quickly at home. An added bonus is that this dessert is made with coconut milk, which is very nourishing. I like to make this for my family because my daughter has sensitivities to milk, and I want her to feel like she can enjoy the same things as everyone else. It doesn't feel like a substitute at all– this ice cream is very luxurious and indulgent.

Ingredients

A can of full-fat coconut milk

1-2 3.5 oz (100 gram) 70% dark chocolate bars

You choose how much chocolate you want to use-- if you are more of a milk-chocolate fan, then go for one, if you like it darker, then use more! I used 1 1/2 for mine, and you will soon see just how chocolatey it looks.

You will also need an ice cream machine and a saucepan or milk scalder.

Instructions

Empty half of your can of coconut milk into a saucepan or milk scalder.

Break your chocolate bar into pieces, and add it to the coconut milk.

Heat the mixture over low heat, stirring frequently. Just get it warm enough to melt the chocolate.

Add the remaining coconut milk and blend it together by stirring.

Pour your mixture into the ice cream machine! Let that machine do its thing, and then either eat as soft-serve, or put in a glass container in the freezer to solidify.

# Lemon & Honey Greek Frozen Yogurt

This is literally one of the simplest recipes I know. And it's incredibly good. When we first made this at home, we repeated the process about every other day for a month– we just couldn't get enough of it.

This frozen yogurt is so quick, and super clean and refreshing. I've served it as a perfect dessert when we had guests over for brunch. (Serves 6)

Ingredients

3 cups full-fat plain Greek yogurt

1/4 cup honey

the zest and juice of one organic lemon

you will need an ice cream maker

Instructions

In a bowl, mix the honey into the yogurt and stir until completely blended.

Add the lemon juice and zest, and give a quick stir.

Pour the yogurt mixture into the ice cream machine, and let it work its magic. Enjoy!

Drinks

We are a family that usually drinks water, but we also love special drinks for enhancing a meal or adding a celebratory note to any moment.

I love making special drinks for my family, and try to tie them into various events. We love to have sangria (and "kid sangria") on warm summer evenings, hot chocolate for special breakfasts, and of course wine and ciders and beers and homemade probiotic sodas to add something special to our dinners or Saturday afternoon lunches and picnics.

Only in the last few years have we started making our own home-brewed alcoholic drinks and fermented sodas, and it's been so cool to learn and experiment! Not only is it a whole lot of fun, but we are able to enjoy truly unique, delicious drinks that are more wholesome and satisfying than the store-bought varieties.

Here are some of our favorite drinks, and the sodas and home-brews I share are some of my simplest recipes that require minimal experience or equipment.

# Sangria

Sangria is the answer to all of your summertime beverage problems. Watch, I'll show you: Is it too hot? *Sangria.* Is that bottle of wine you opened a week ago no longer drinkable? *Sangria.* Cheap wine? Lousy wine? *Sangria.* Fresh summer fruit fading fast? *Sangria.* Need a drink that will go far at a party? *Sangria.* Need a mixed drink that will keep for a week in the fridge? *Sangria.*

See? Sangria is the best. I have been making it regularly ever since I learned how from the owner of the little bistro I was working at 12 years ago. People started requesting that I make it for their parties, and it's been my go-to for every summer gathering. I've made a few different versions, and this drink is so adaptable that there are infinite ways to make it. If I'm being super-honest, I like my own sangria more than any I've had in restaurants– they tend to be way too sweet, and a little cheap on the fruit flavors. I'll share with you the recipe that I like the most, and you can take it from there. (Makes about 4 quarts)

## Ingredients

1 bottle of red wine and 1 bottle of white wine
This can seriously be the cheapest wine on the shelf. Do not waste a great bottle of wine this way, but you can also use a good bottle that has been open too long– it's a great way to save it!

2 organic oranges, sliced thinly into rounds

1 bag of frozen mixed berries– preferably with some cherries in it, too.

1/2 cup triple sec or cointreau or brandy
(And yes, I have successfully made sangria without any of these– but it really is worth it if you can get some!)

1 quart of cherry juice, and using cherry juice concentrate (diluted) is an economical way to go (optional, but recommended)

fresh strawberries and/ or other dark-colored fruits (again, optional if you have plenty of frozen berries– but this is a great way to use those strawberries that are languishing in the heat)

## Instructions

Well, you pretty much just get a huge glass container and mix all of these things (besides the ice) together. Stir it up, and taste. Depending on the wine you are using, you may feel the need to make it a little sweeter. You can use sugar, brown sugar, or raw honey (diluted with water so that it will dissolve in the cold mixture).

If possible, let it sit for an hour or more so the flavors can marry. It would be totally reasonable to leave it overnight, if you want.

Serve over ice, and garnish if you like with orange slices or fresh strawberries. Use a ladle to get the berries from the bottom, so there's a bit of everything in each glass.

Be sure to enjoy the wine-soaked fruits at the bottom of your glass!

Easy. Delicious. Fresh. *Sangria!*

And, if you manage to save some, you can put your leftovers in the fridge for tomorrow! *Lucky you.*

# Kid Sangria

We do our best not to leave Amelia out of the fun when it comes to drinks. Lately, we've been making home-made fermented sodas, which are great (and perhaps a subject of a future cookbook). But these take some time. "Kid Sangria" has always been a big hit, and can be made instantly. I also like this because the fruit juice can be as diluted as you want it to be, without compromising on style and flavor because of the fruit in the drink.

Of course, this also works for grownups! Perfect for a hot summer afternoon, when you're not looking to get dehydrated by an alcoholic drink.

Ingredients

sparkling water

cherry juice (or another kind of fruit juice)
cut up fruit, especially berries and slices of oranges (I like to keep frozen fruit on hand for this)

a squeeze of orange juice

Instructions

Mix everything together. Taste and see if it's balanced to your liking, and adjust.

Garnish with a little slice of orange on the side of the glass.

# Fermented Blackberry Soda

Fermented fruit sodas are so fun to make, simple, and delicious. You can use this method for any fruit, really, and it's very easily adapted to various fruits and types of sugar.

This recipe does require a few pieces of home brewing equipment. Since we make a lot of our own beverages, this is not an issue for me-- but one one-gallon demijohn and an airlock and some bottles are a very small investment toward lots of wonderful homemade probiotic sodas for your family.

This method is pretty loose, and feel free to adjust the ingredient measurements.

In the warmer months, I like to keep fermented sodas on hand. It's a nice treat in the afternoon, and something to offer Amelia when we're enjoying our home-brewed beers and wines. They are so refreshing, and I can't get over the fun of creating really fizzy drinks through some simple kitchen chemistry.

Ingredients

5 cups blackberries– either fresh or frozen

3/4 cup raw, local honey or sugar– brown sugar or evaporated cane juice would be nice

some kind of culture– you can use sauerkraut juice or whey from strained yogurt– you only need a tablespoon or two

In terms of equipment, you will need a demijohn, an airlock, a funnel and swing-top bottles. A big glass cider jug is perfect to use as a demijohn.

The type of bottle is important, as they allow the ferment to give off some small amounts of carbon dioxide and won't explode.

(Some people have had success with putting a balloon over the top of the demijohn with a pin hole in the top to mimic an airlock. Worth a try in a pinch!)

Instructions

Put the blackberries into a pot, and cover with 8 cups of water. Bring to a simmer.

Simmer for about 30 minutes over low heat, then cool.

Strain out the blackberries.

Add the honey or sugar and stir until dissolved. Taste it. Keep in mind that the sugars will be digested to create the fizz, so you do want to start with it much sweeter than you would like the soda to be. Add more sugar if needed.

Pour the "juice" into a sterilized or very clean demijohn, add your whey or sauerkraut juice and add your airlock.

Let it sit for about three days, and taste it. Mine ferments pretty quickly, but there are some variables– the temperature of the room, the strength of the culture you used, etc. Taste it and let it ferment until it's only a little sweeter than you would like it to be.

Pour it into your swing-top bottles, and store in the fridge. You could leave them out at room temperature if you'd like to drink them sooner, but I usually pop them into the fridge to slow down the fermentation process. You will want to drink them within a few weeks, or risk losing most of your Blackberry Soda to the "geyser effect." If you're storing it for a while, I'd just check in now and then to see what kind of pressure is building up.

Your beverage will get drier, more tart and fizzier the longer you wait. It will eventually develop more of an alcohol content, too, so you might want to taste it before giving it to your kids if you've been storing it for a while!

Enjoy!

# Nature Reserves & Foraging in England

**If I could name one thing that I am the most in love with about England, it would be *the land*.** As I have mentioned many times, one of our simplest pleasures is going for a drive in the country that surrounds us. It's just beautiful, despite the fact that most of it is privately owned farmland. But there are also SO many special places all around us that are under the care of the National Wildlife Trust.

These places are wonderful, and incredibly accessible. Recently, Jeff had the day off, so we made it a date and we visited Lackford Lakes– only about a 20 minute drive from us. This piece of land used to be a gravel pit before it was donated to the Suffolk Wildlife Trust. It was restored, and has become a rich nature reserve with meadows, woodland, reed beds, streams and pond, attracting a very diverse bird population. We visited at this time of the year last autumn, and enjoyed eating tons of blackberries.

This time, Jeff and I brought a basket, to bring home some of the bounty. (Another thing I love about the reserves here is that foraging is absolutely permitted, under some very reasonable guidelines.) Honestly, we didn't cover a whole lot of territory, since there were ripe blackberries *everywhere* we turned. We picked about six to eight cups-worth. We also found a more limited selection of elderberries! These were extremely easy to pick, as we could just snap off the stems full of shiny, round fruit jewels.

It was a very pleasant afternoon spent quietly picking berries and listening to the ducks cackling and hundreds of birds twittering. Being in a place like that is incredibly therapeutic and nurturing to my spirit. I don't take the easy access for granted.

I noticed that there are also a ton of rosehips ripening. They weren't ready to pick yet, but we kept them on our radar for the upcoming weeks.

When we came home, I made a winter tonic with the elderberries, cooking them down with fresh ginger, cinnamon and cloves, then adding some raw Suffolk honey. We used to pay a fortune for elderberry syrup in Portland, and it is incredibly satisfying to make our own medicine at home.

As for the blackberries, I cooked them down, and made a Fermented Blackberry Soda (page 136), as well as a grown-up drink, similar to old-school ginger beer. Both were wonderful, and it was such a treat to make them from fruits growing locally. **I often wonder if people who grew up here have any idea just how lucky they are… Do you think they do?**

# Fermented Rhubarb & Honey Soda

Rhubarb Soda is a lot of fun– it's a very pretty pink and fizzy drink, kind of like lemonade, with a rosy flavor– so nice! Plus… Probiotics! What a nice way to get some more into your family. As with most home fermentation projects, this formula is flexible.

This soda is lightly sweet and exotic, tart and so refreshing– and not to mention the pleasures of a *pink* beverage. Plus, there is something really exciting about making your own intense carbonation, naturally. That always gives me a thrill. I hope you'll try making some– it's really very easy, and you can't buy anything like it!

Ingredients

6 stalks of rhubarb, or about 4 cups, chopped into 1/2 inch pieces

about 3/4 cup raw, local honey, or you can also use sugar instead

some kind of culture– you can use sauerkraut juice or whey from strained yogurt– you only need a tablespoon or two

In terms of equipment, you will need a demijohn, an airlock, a funnel and swing-top bottles. A big glass cider jug is perfect to use as a demijohn.

The type of bottle is important, as they allow the ferment to give off some small amounts of carbon dioxide and won't explode.

(Some people have had success with putting a balloon over the top of the demijohn with a pin hole in the top to mimic an airlock. Worth a try in a pinch!)

Instructions

Put the rhubarb into a large pot, and cover with about 8 cups of water. Bring to a simmer. Cook until the rhubarb is very tender, then cool. You can leave yours overnight, if you'd like.

Strain out the rhubarb. Add the honey and stir until dissolved. Taste. Dilute the syrup with water if it comes on too strong (if it's too tart, since it will get more sour as it ferments).

Pour the "juice" into a sterilized demijohn, add your whey or sauerkraut juice and add your airlock.

Let it sit for about three days, and taste it. Length of time can vary, related to the temperature of the room, the strength of the culture you used, type of sugar, etc.

Taste it and let it ferment until it's only a little sweeter than you would like it to be.

Pour it into your swing-top bottles, and store in the fridge. You could leave them out at room temperature if you'd like to drink them sooner, but I usually pop them into the fridge to slow down the fermentation process. You will want to drink them within a week, or risk losing most of your Rhubarb Soda to the "geyser effect." Your beverage will get drier, more tart and fizzier the longer you wait. It will eventually develop more of an alcohol content, too, so you might want to taste it before giving it to your kids if you've been storing it for a while!

# Coffee Frappe

I am a little embarrassed to call this a recipe, but I'll get over that hangup so I can make your summer afternoons that much better.

So, you may not know that coffee becomes incredibly light and creamy when you blend it up with ice. I did not know this until two summers ago, and it was a real game-changer. Apparently, a coffee frappe is a super popular drink in Greece– but it's made with instant coffee! *I can't do that*. So this may not be an authentic Greek Coffee Frappe, but it *is* the perfect afternoon pick-me-up, and a great way to use up leftover coffee.

Ingredients

coffee-- an espresso or even an Americano works particularly well, but strong brewed coffee will do the trick

ice

a little sweetener like brown sugar, optional

a blender

Instructions

Do I really have to say it? OK.

Just blend the coffee up with the ice, and add the sweetener. Blend and blend, until the ice is obliterated into slush and the whole thing is foamy.

Enjoy!

# Simple Apple Peel Cider

One day last fall, I had spent all morning in the kitchen making a colossal batch of apple sauce. It's not that we're huge apple sauce eaters, but that there were a ton of apple trees in our area dropping their fruit– and no one else seemed to be picking them up! So we brought home a couple big bags full, and I set to work peeling and coring them.

I saved the peels, thinking there must be something I could use them for. I thought about an apple peel wine, but never found any compelling recipes or posts about making it– plus, the one I did find called for a list of things that I didn't want to have to get. I just wanted to do something quick and simple. So, I thought I'd just do my own thing and see what would happen. I made Apple Peel Cider. And now I am happy to share that the experiment was a success, and you can try it, too!

The cool thing about cider is that you can make it without adding any yeast. The skins of the apples have the yeast culture on them already. This makes things somewhat unpredictable, though, since you don't know exactly what it will taste like. But that's something I really love about wild-culturing– the element of surprise.

# Making Simple Apple Peel Cider

Please understand that this is not a typical, structured, exact recipe. I want to tell you how I made my Apple Peel Cider, roughly, and then let you have your own fun experiment with your apple scraps. It's totally interesting, and not much work– why not have a go, right?

Start with organic, unwaxed apples. The best ones are not from the supermarket, but ones you know the origins of somewhat– a local orchard, your farmer's market, or a neighborhood tree. This is the perfect project for doing after you have processed a bunch of apples for something else– apple sauce, pie fillings, preserves, etc. Save your peels (cores too, if they are not too funky– but avoid the big moldy patches you have to cut out of windfall apples). Collect all of your peels.

Put them in a fermentation bucket, and pour boiling water over them. I used about equal parts water to peels by volume (not weight). I added some chunks of peeled fresh ginger, and recommend it, if you like ginger too. (I had no trouble with developing the yeast this way, but you might want to keep a handful of peels out of the boiling water, and add them once the mixture has cooled, to be 100% sure that you don't kill all of the yeast with the hot water.)

Cover the apple peels and water with lid, and let everything sit for 3-4 days. This will allow the yeast to develop and begin fermenting the apples. Tip: To ensure that you have a good yeast, just buy a cider yeast from a brew shop, or order it online. Not everyone likes the flavor of their local wild yeast, and in some cases the yeast has been washed off of the apples. I use wild, but it's not hard at all to add a sachet of cider yeast from a brewing supply shop (or online) instead.

Strain the liquid from the peels, and add sugar. I used organic natural sugar, and added about a cup to one gallon of liquid. The formula for a stronger cider is more sugar + more time = higher alcohol content. I wasn't going for a super strong drink, and the result has been really light, tart and fresh.

Pour the cider mixture into sterilized demijohns, put the airlock on, and let it do its thing

somewhere away from the cold for two weeks. You can of course taste after one week, and see where you're at. If the cider is already drier than you want, then you can add some sugar. Again, this is very experimental, and is a virtually free science project that will yield a fun home brew!

When it's just slightly sweeter than what you want, it's time to bottle. Be sure to use swing-top bottles, because the is a fizzy drink and will burst regular bottles if there isn't a mechanism to release small amounts of CO2 when it builds up.

Open a bottle within a couple of days, and see what it's doing. If you like where your cider's at, then put the other bottles in the fridge to slow down the fermentation process, and drink sooner rather than later. This will continue to ferment, and you may get a more champagne-like product than you want, if you leave it for too long. The over-fermented version usually tastes awesome, but you are likely to lose most of it to the geyser-effect when you open the bottle. (Yes, I am very familiar with this part!) Enjoy your free, one-of-a-kind autumn drinks!

# Glühwein

The little Victorian row house we inhabit now in England is full of charm... And full of cracks, where the cold winds blow right in, in winter time. We don't want an astronomical heating bill, and we have already asked our landlord to do some weatherizations... And while we wait, we don extra socks, sweaters, jackets and wool blankets. And we make Glühwein.

Few things really warm you up from the inside, out like this delicious, warm, spiced wine– and luckily, it's really simple to make. Every sip I take brings me back to the Christmas we spent in Germany, and the wonderfully cozy Christmas market in our little town of Amberg. People out and about in the evenings, crunching through thick blankets of snow, drinking Glühwein and eating Leibkuchen or Bratwurst. Sigh... I am afraid Germany has ruined us for Christmas anywhere else in the world. And while we are here wishing we could visit a Christmas market, we enjoy sips of it in the form of this delicious mulled wine. And now you can, too!

## Ingredients

1 (750 milliliter) bottle red wine
(This is a great use of a cheaper wine, or one that you were disappointed with!)

3/4 cup water

1/2 cup honey or sugar

1 cinnamon stick

1 organic orange

10 whole cloves

orange liqueur, brandy or rum– all optional

## Instructions

Pour the water into a saucepan over medium heat, and bring to a boil. Add the honey.

Poke the cloves into the skin of the orange, slice into halves, and squeeze some of the juice into the water, and throw in the clove-studded peels. Add the cinnamon, and let this mixture simmer and reduce until it begins to thicken. Your house will smell *amazing*. Pour the wine in, and heat very gently, until it begins steaming. Don't boil the wine! Remove the orange peels and cinnamon stick.

Serve in mugs, adding a shot of the orange liqueur, brandy or rum, if you need a little extra heat. I always ordered mine *"mit einem Schuss Brandy."* Enjoy the coziness that will inevitably creep all the way down to your toes.

To make this as a gift, just make room in the bottle of wine to pour in a batch of the syrup, put the cork back on it, and then add a festive label with instructions to heat the wine. It will keep for a couple of weeks.

# The Christmas Market in Germany

Our first Thanksgiving in Germany was difficult for us. In fact, I couldn't even bring myself to cook a Thanksgiving dinner– because it made my heart sick to eat it without family. So while dear ones at home were cooking their holiday meals, we were out celebrating the beginning of the Christmas season.

Thanksgiving day worked out to be the first night of the Christmas markets, which open one month before Christmas Day. It's incredibly fun and festive and cozy. The timing could not have been more perfect for us.

Amelia and her fellow kindergartners had the privilege of opening up the festivities with songs on a stage in the middle of the town square. It was really sweet. There was also a lady standing up there with the traditional wreath with little candles in it on her head (Amelia told me the name for it, but I've forgotten!). They sang a few songs, including "Nikolaus" which is sung to the same tune as "Jingle Bells."

There was quite a lot of fanfare, and afterward we had fun milling around, looking at shops, enjoying warm drinks. There were also roasted chestnuts and carousel rides! Everyone was cheerful and friendly, and it was fun to see the whole town out together.

And of course, the main attraction was the Cider/ Glühwein booth. In Germany, they serve you your drink in a real mug (no plastic or styrofoam) and you pay a little deposit on the cup. When you're done at the end of the evening, you get your money back. I love this– so little waste, and I feel much more at home drinking from a real mug– more like I'm at someone's home than at a public event!

I think we fit right in.

I loved all of the booths selling their wares. I especially enjoyed the *Krippe* shop— selling anything and everything you could possibly think of for a nativity scene. I can only assume that people there set up elaborate towns each year… The miniature home goods are my favorite, especially the straw brooms! And you cannot forget the beehives, birdhouses, rabbit hutches and wells!

There were a lot of stores selling Christmas decorations. My favorite ones are the woodland creatures, made out of woodland materials.

Of course, there were plenty of sweets shops. These are *Lebkuchen*— gingerbread cookies!

One of the best things about being at the Christmas market was the fact that there were plenty of people around that we knew.

Even though it had only been a few months since we moved to Amberg, I had made a lot of relationships with parents of the kids at Amelia's school, and so our family felt like we were actual participants, rather than observers. That was truly heart-warming for me!

# Coconut Milk & Ginger Hot Chocolate

This is the marriage of two taste memories I carry around from my childhood in the Philippines. We had cacao trees in our garden when I was a kid. We would crack open the pods to get to the fuzzy white seeds, and suck that sweet fruit off of them. Then the seeds would be laid in the sun to dry, then roasted, and the thin husks would come off. Then they could be taken into the market to be milled into chocolate. Most of the time, we did not make our own chocolate, but bought it at the market in little discs about the size of a silver dollar and half an inch thick, called *tablea*. We would add these to hot water and whisk for a thick chocolate drink, mixed with coconut milk and sugar. So delicious. My parents still send me *tablea* from the Philippines every year.

The other half of the nostalgia for this drink is all about hot ginger. You can buy a crystallized powdered ginger (*salabat*) drink at the supermarket in the Philippines. Just add hot water and stir it up for a sweet, spicy drink. I used to go over to our land lady's home in the afternoons when she came home from work, for this afternoon ritual. Mrs. Espiritu worked in a government office, but had a baking business on the side, which I often helped with. She would pick up fresh *pan de sal* on her way home, and we would sit at her table and fill them with the custard fillings she had made for cakes, and enjoy cups of hot ginger tea with added evaporated milk. I don't know if this sounds good to you or not, but I loved it. I get pretty wistful about hot ginger, even if I cringe a little thinking about how sweet that store-bought blend was.

I like to combine these two memories in my own nostalgic hot drink. It's become a tradition for me to make this gingery hot chocolate every Christmas morning for my family.

To make the hot chocolate, I use Filipino pure cacao tablets. But you could use Abuelita or Ibarra brand Mexican hot chocolate wedges. They already have cinnamon and sugar added, so you won't need to add any.

Follow instructions on the box, and make it with half (full fat) coconut milk and half water.
Add 1/4 teaspoon of powdered ginger, and a pinch of salt per serving. I sometimes add cayenne powder, too.

Use an immersion blender to get it nicely mixed. If you have any, you could also add 1/2 teaspoon of grass-fed gelatin powder-- not only is it really good for you, but it adds an extra thickness which I love.

151

Basics

Over the years, I have had the joy of helping some brand new cooks find their way in the kitchen. It can be really intimidating to go from boxed foods to using whole ingredients, turning all of these pieces into a real meal. There are a few things that I like to introduce first, which will make everything easier after that.

For example, the very first protein I teach someone to cook is a whole roasted chicken. This can then be broken down-- meat reserved for soups and other leftovers, and the bones are used to make a wonderfully rich and nourishing broth.

Another thing we eat a lot of is fermented foods. Making sauerkraut is easy, and it's a great way to build your family's immune system– plus, it's great to have it on hand as a side dish to liven up most meals you serve.

So in this section, I'd like to show you some of the basics that I think every cook should know.

# Whole Roasted Chicken with Lemon & Rosemary

Roasting a whole chicken is one of the first things a home cook should learn, in my opinion. First of all, it's really much simpler than you'd expect, with a confidence-inspiring presentation at the end. It fills your home with warm, delicious smells, and then provides you with another meal or two after you've eaten your succulent chicken dinner.

This is a very basic recipe, and one that I hope you will create your own variations of. One thing you can also do to switch it up is to use one of the marinades on page 75 to rub on the skin of the chicken, adding similar spices with the lemon wedges and garlic to the inside of the chicken– so delicious!

Ingredients

1 (5 to 6 pound) roasting chicken

coarse sea salt

black pepper, freshly cracked

several sprigs of fresh rosemary

1 organic lemon, halved

4 cloves garlic, peeled and crushed roughly

2 tablespoons butter, melted

1 large yellow onion, peeled and sliced into quarters

4 carrots, scrubbed and cut into 2-inch chunks

olive oil

you will need a roasting pan

Instructions

Preheat the oven to 425° F (220°C).

Remove the chicken giblets, if there are any, and set aside for making chicken stock.

Liberally salt and pepper the inside of the chicken. Stuff the cavity with the fresh rosemary, lemon halves, and the garlic. (I like to alternate these a bit, and end with a lemon half, helping to keep the rest inside the bird.)

Massage the outside of the chicken with the melted butter and sprinkle again with salt and pepper. An optional step is to tie the legs together with kitchen string and tuck the wing tips under the body of the chicken.

Put the veggies in a roasting pan. Toss with salt, pepper, and a drizzle of olive oil. Spread around the bottom of the roasting pan and place the chicken on top. Roast the chicken for 1 1/2 hours, or until the juices run clear when you cut between a leg and thigh.

Remove the chicken and vegetables to a platter and cover with aluminum foil for about 20 minutes, to let it finish cooking and to let the juices settle. Carve the chicken and serve it with the vegetables. Save any remains from the roasting pan to add into the chicken stock.

# How to Cook a Flank Steak

I consider this one a basic because it really is one of the quickest, easiest ways that you can cook beef. A flank steak is inexpensive and flavorful, and although marinating it is a great idea, a flank steak can also be cooked without anything but freshly cracked pepper and some sea salt.

I try to pick up a flank steak from my butcher once a week, and it's my "emergency" meal– for those days when I haven't planned ahead, feel lazy (yes, it happens!) or don't have time to do much cooking. It's done in 15 minutes, and I can just throw together a salad, and steam some potatoes or veggies to go with it, and I'm done.

Ingredients

a medium-sized flank steak, between 1-2 pounds

2 tablespoons marinade (optional)

sea salt

fresh pepper

1 tablespoon bacon grease, beef tallow or avocado oil to grease the pan

for equipment, you'll need a cast-iron skillet or a grill pan to cook on the stovetop (or you can use an actual grill) and some kitchen tongs

Instructions

(Optional) Pour marinade over your flank steak and rub it in so it's covering all of the meat. Let sit in the fridge for 1-2 hours, or overnight.

If needed, cut your steak in half to fit into your skillet or grill pan.

Heat the skillet over medium heat for a minute, and then add the fat you will cook with.

Dry the steaks off well with a kitchen towel or paper towels

Fry the steaks on each side for approximately 3 minutes for medium-rare doneness. Cook for 4 minutes on each side if you want it to reach medium doneness. You really don't want your meat well-done, and it will become tough.

Remove the skirt steaks from the heat, and set them on a cutting board. Allow the meat to rest for at least 5 to 10 minutes before serving.

Cut them against the grain of the meat, into very thin slices. I like to top mine with Chimichurri Sauce (page 66) or Herbed Compound Butter (page 58) if un-marinated.

# How to Make Chicken Stock

When I first started cooking, I always wondered how to get really rich, flavorful soups. Most of mine just tasted like the water I used to make them with. When I began making my own broths, everything changed.

Bone broths are the foundation of nourishing meals at our house. I make either a pot of chicken stock or beef stock most weeks of the year, and sometimes both during the winter. They add wonderful flavor, thickness, and nourishment to most of our meals. I use them when steaming veggies and making

## Ingredients

one roasted chicken carcass-- cooked meat removed for use in soups and other meals

5 sticks celery, roughly chopped (optional)

2 medium leeks, roughly chopped (optional)

2 medium onions, roughly chopped

2 large carrots, roughly chopped

3 bay leaves

5 whole black peppercorns

4 quarts cold water

1/4 cup apple cider vinegar

for equipment, you will need a good-sized stock pot and a sieve

## Instructions

Place the chicken carcass, vegetables, bay leaves and peppercorns in the stock pot.

Add the cold water and bring to the boil. Skim any froth off the top, then turn the heat down to a simmer.

Continue to simmer gently for at least 4 hours, and up to 24 hours, replenishing water and skimming as necessary. After the first couple of hours, add the vinegar-- this helps to pull the minerals and healing gelatin from the bones.

Strain into jars, allow to cool for about half an hour, then refrigerate.

I often pour it into muffin tins and freeze it, then put the discs into a freezer bag for easy use as needed.

It will keep in the fridge for about 4 days and in the freezer for 2-3 months.

# How to Make Beef Stock

Although I had seen my mom making chicken stock many times as a kid (she boiled the whole bird, and it was my job to pull the meat off the chicken) I had no idea how beef broth was made until I read about it in Nourishing Traditions, a really educational cookbook.

I now regularly ask my butcher for any and all beef bones he can give me, so I can keep my fridge and freezer well-stocked with this fantastic elixir.

## Ingredients

4 pounds of beef bones– marrow bones and, knuckle bones or whatever you can get your hands on

3 pounds meaty rib or neck bones

4 or more quarts cold water

1/4 cup red wine vinegar or cider vinegar

3 onions, coarsely chopped

3 carrots, scrubbed and coarsely chopped

4 bay leaves

10 black peppercorns

## Instructions

Place all of your bones that have meaty bits on them in a roasting pan and roast in the oven at 350° F (180° C) until well-browned, about 30- 45 minutes.

Meanwhile, throw all of your non-meaty bones into your stockpot, and add the water, vegetables, bay leaves and pepper. Let this sit while the other bones are browning.

Add the browned bones to the pot, including any juices or brown bits from the roasting pan. Add additional water if needed to cover the bones, and bring to a boil.

Remove any scum/foam that rises to the top. Reduce heat, cover and simmer for at least 12 hours and as long as 72 hours. The longer you cook the stock, the more rich and flavorful it will be.

Remove the bones with a slotted spoon and/or tongs. Strain the stock into any vessels (like mason jars) that you are using to store it in.

Let the jars cool, then freeze or refrigerate.

It will keep in the fridge for about a week and in the freezer for 2-3 months.

# How to Make Your Own Sauerkraut

Saurerkraut is one of those foods that I never developed a taste for until adulthood– but now both my husband and I really crave it, if we haven't had it in a while. I like to make huge batches at a time, that will last my family for months.

Sauerkraut is a fantastic source of probiotics, and is really great for digestion. It has a pleasant sourness, and when you make it at home, you have the chance to get it just how you like it best. This ferment is kind of the gateway into home-fermentation wonderland. Lots of people begin with sauerkraut, and then can't stop until they've tried to ferment every veggie they can get their hands on. (Ahem, not that I would know!)

After you make your first batch or two, you should definitely begin experimenting with adding other elements-- like spices, herbs and other vegetables. My favorite concoction includes cumin, coriander, nigella, chili flakes and fenugreek. (Makes 2 quarts, roughly)

Ingredients

2 heads cabbage-- one red and one green (you could use all-green, but the pink color you get from using red is really wonderful)

2 tablespoons coarse sea salt

1-2 tablespoons caraway seeds (optional)

in terms of equipment, you'll need a food processor, a cutting board, a chef's knife, a large mixing bowl, mason jars (enough to house 2 quarts, with an inch of headspace left in each) and snack-sized ziplock bags

Instructions

Start by giving your workspace, hands, and equipment a really thorough cleaning-- this is important.

Remove the limp outer leaves of the cabbage, and set them aside to use later.

Cut the cabbage into quarters, and put through the food processor, using the shredding disc.

Move the grated cabbage to the mixing bowl, and add the salt. Working the salt into the cabbage by massaging and squeezing the cabbage with your hands. It will gradually begin oozing a bit of cabbage juice, and this is exactly what you want. If your hands get tired, you can also start pounding the cabbage with the bottom of a (very clean) wine bottle. Do this for at least 5 minutes.

Add any spices, like the caraway seeds.

Now you're ready to put the cabbage into its jars. Take handfuls and stuff them in, periodically tamping the kraut down with your fist or a wooden spoon.

Once the cabbage is in its jar(s) pour any liquid released by the cabbage over it.

Now take one or two of the outer leaves you removed and set aside, and use it to cover the cabbage and press it down. It's important to keep all of the vegetable submerged through the fermentation process, and this really helps!

If the liquid level does not come over the top cabbage leaf, then you need to add some more water.

Fill the snack-sized ziplock bag with water, and put it in the jar, to help bring the liquid level to the top. This is what you're using in place of a traditional weight or stone.

At this point, some people cover the jar with a clean cloth. If you have bugs where you are keeping your ferment, then this is probably a good idea. On my kitchen counter, it's not an issue, and I leave it open during this part.

Let it sit for a full day, and press down now and then to keep everything submerged. I put my jars on a dish or a pan, so any overflow is caught. If the liquid level is too low, add some salty water.

Ferment the cabbage for 3 to 10 days, ideally at a room temperature between 65°F to 75°F.

Check it now and then, pressing it down if the cabbage is floating above the liquid.

A small batch like this will ferment fairly quickly. Start tasting it after four days. It's up to you how sour you like it, so you decide when it's done. A little white scum or residue on top is perfectly fine, and if you see a little mold, remove it right away and make sure your cabbage is submerged.

Sauerkraut will keep for months in the fridge.

# Making a Vegetable Puree

Vegetable purees are a serious staple at our table, and they are a fantastic option for grain-free cooking, since you can make them so quickly and easily with whatever you have on hand. They are delicious and filling, and easily qualify as comfort food.

The following instructions are more technique than recipe, as there are all kinds of right ways to do this, once you learn the basics of making a vegetable puree. If you'd like to start with a more specific recipe, then the Celeriac & Apple Puree (page 38) will be perfect.

## Ingredients

root vegetables, cauliflower, or winter squash, peeled and roughly chopped (hint: if using a combination of veggies, then chop the firmer ones smaller so they will cook at roughly the same rate as the other veggies)

chicken, beef, or vegetable stock

butter

lemon juice

salt

pepper

in terms of equipment, you will need a large pot with a lid and an immersion blender

## Instructions

Put your vegetables in your pot, pour about 2 inches of stock in, and cover.

Cook over medium heat for about 15 minutes, and check veggies to see if they are tender. Once they become fork-tender, remove from heat. Pour off any remaining liquid, and reserve.

Add butter, a squeeze of lemon juice, some salt and pepper. Puree until smooth, then taste. If it's too thick, use some of the reserved liquid to thin it out, and blend some more.

Adjust seasonings (salt, pepper, lemon juice and even butter) until it tastes exactly how you like it to.

I usually make as much as I can at a time, so I can simply reheat and serve for another meal. This also freezes well.

# On Going Grain—Free

There are a lot of different reasons that people decide to switch to a grain-free diet, and I know it can be really helpful for a lot of people. Some hardly have a choice– their own health or that of their child is suffering, and things have got to change, *now*. I get it. I also understand that it can be pretty challenging. When we made the switch to a grain-free diet, I was already cooking around multiple allergies. Having to avoid corn, soy, gluten and dairy had already kept me on my toes, so simply eliminating grains as a food group felt like simplifying our lives, in many ways. We've been doing this for over four years now, and I promise you that it does get better. *Much* better.

I know that a lot of people are met with, "But what can you eat?!" when they first tell someone that they are no longer eating grains. It's kind of a silly question, because there are tons of things to eat. Delicious things. Easy things. Awesome things.

The main challenge is simply replacing grain-rich foods you are used to relying on, and having a list of go-to foods that you can keep on hand easily.

Here are some of my best tips for making the transition to grain-free smoothly.

1. First of all, I just want to point out that omitting grains will not cause any nutritional deficiencies. In fact, it will really increase your overall nutrition. I know people talk a lot about "healthy whole grains" but what you'll actually be eating more of now is vegetables. And we all know vegetables are very nutrient rich. Moreover, most of the foods you'll be eating (meats, nuts, eggs, etc.) have even more of the nutrients you would get from grains.

2. Vegetables are where it's at. If you are wondering how to make a satisfying, well-rounded meal, think veggies. They can be prepared so many different ways, and are an awesome starch substitute in many cases. Here are some of my favorite ways to use them in place of other grains or starches:

    - Cauliflower rice in place of regular rice
    - Zucchini noodles (aka zoodles) instead of regular pasta (seriously tasty, I promise!)
    - Baked spaghetti squash in place of angel hair pasta
    - Cabbage ribbons in brothy Asian soups and curries
    - Lettuce cups for serving tuna salad and chicken salad
    - Blanched whole cabbage leaves as wraps for tacos
    - Sliced and grilled eggplant as a pita bread substitute
    - Root vegetable or cauliflower purees in place of mashed potatoes, for those of you cutting down on starches
    - Roasted sweet potatoes as a replacement for any type of starch

3. Change your meal framework. Instead of thinking of having a protein, a vegetable and a starch, just opt for more vegetables, and different textures and colors on your plate. Sometimes we have a flank steak and just a salad, or sometimes we do flank steak, steamed and buttered veggies, *and* roasted sweet potatoes. Don't get stuck on meals needing to fit a certain format.

4. Ethnic foods are your new best friend. A lot of Asian, Middle Eastern and Mediterranean foods are naturally grain-free. Choosing an authentic ethnic restaurant is one of the best choices when eating out, and we even find that we have very little problem with avoiding grains when we're in places like France and Belgium.

5. Don't get hung up on replacements. I think that switching to a different diet gets *more* frustrating if you are constantly trying to recreate traditional meals from your grain-loving days. It's so much easier to pick great meals that don't have grains in them to begin with. I do get a craving for pizza now and then, but making a paleo crust has been more trouble than it's worth, most of the time. Go ahead and put the

work in if you are *really* craving a favorite food that you miss, but don't plan your menus around it.

In terms of desserts, why not just make a good flourless chocolate cake, rather than worrying about a substitute for a traditional chocolate cake? Or do a good flan or creme brulee or ice cream, etc. There are so many great foods out there that simply don't include grains.

6. That said, there are great recipes out there for just about anything you could possibly crave, including biscuits, hamburger buns, and sandwich bread. And cake. (For example, my Parsnip & Carrot Cake!) So while building your menus around substitute foods is not the easiest way to go, know that you can probably scratch that itch when you really need to– the internet is a beautiful thing!

7. Eggs, nuts, and coconut are your friends. Keep your cupboards and fridge stocked with staples like plenty of eggs, almond flour, coconut flour, grated coconut and coconut milk. You can make all sorts of comfort foods with these. If I am ever feeling tired of the typical savory morning fare, I love to whip up a Grain-Free Dutch Baby. All of these things are nourishing and filling, and you can make some great, quick snacks with them.

8. A big issue for a lot of people who are cutting out grains is sugar/ starch cravings. The best way to work with this is to increase your fat intake. It's satiating and will really help with those cravings, I promise. Personally, I like to treat myself to dark chocolate, with a spoonful of almond butter and a little sea salt.

9. Cook extra. Whenever you can, make more. This will save you so much time and energy. Even if you aren't making enough for an entire meal the next day, just having extra food on hand will be helpful. I try to have extra proteins available, as that can be the trickiest thing to find when I need a good snack: extra Chelo Kebabs, roasted chicken slices, hard-boiled eggs, cans of tuna, etc. All of these things also make lunches **much** easier.

10. Shop & prep. One thing you can do to make life easier when you are cooking from scratch is to shop weekly, and then wash and prep your produce all at once. Saturday is our marketing day, and we also visit our butcher. Then we get home and wash all of our produce and put it away. If I can, I take some cauliflower and prep it for cauliflower rice. Do anything you can think of, ahead of time, and it will save you so much time and energy through the week!

# A Typical Week of Groceries and Meals for My Family

I thought it could be really useful to share with you what a week of groceries and meals looks like in our family. I know that for some people, it's just hard to imagine what shopping and eating grain-free or paleo looks like, on a practical level.

So, I thought I'd show you a week's worth of our groceries. This is what we bought on a Saturday, to feed three of us three meals per day, all week.

Our budget is £100 per week, or about $160. Here is everything that this amount bought for us this weekend– from our butcher, a quick stop at Aldi and our favorite farm shop. We spent about £90 on Saturday, leaving us with a little extra for things we need to get during the week.

## A Week of Grain–Free / Paleo Groceries

### Proteins

- 5 dozen eggs
- 4 cans of tuna
- 2.5 lbs. oxtail
- 2 lbs. pork belly
- 1 lb. ground pork
- 2 lbs. ground beef
- a 3 lb. whole chicken
- 2 lbs. stew beef
- 1 chicken carcass for bone broth

### Fats

- 1.5 lbs. butter
- 2 avocados
- sesame seeds

## Vegetables

- 3 hothouse English cucumbers
- 3 lbs. leeks
- 2 heads cauliflower
- 5 lbs. carrots
- 1 bunch beets
- 1.5 lbs zucchini
- 2 fennel bulbs
- 4 heads lettuce
- 1 head of celery
- 1 lb mushrooms
- arugula
- 4 sweet red peppers
- 1 bunch cilantro
- 1 bunch rosemary

## Fruit

- 2.5 lbs pears
- 5 lbs apples

## Misc Grocery

- red wine vinegar
- 2 boxes tomato purée
- giant jar green olives
- small jar black olives
- 1 jar of tahini
- 1 bottle red wine

Of course, it's important to mention that I had some staples at home. Each week, I buy a couple of staples that I won't need to pick up again for a month or two. This week it was maple syrup, sesame seeds, red wine vinegar and green olives. I already had lots of onions, a couple of lemons, sweet potatoes, some winter squash, nuts, coconut oil, coconut milk, garlic, spices, olive oil, chocolate, coffee, etc. in the kitchen. One other thing– the butcher at the farm shop gives me tons of beef bones for free whenever I ask. I still had plenty of beef broth from last week, but I almost always bring home a few pounds of bones for making bone broth.

Also note that we only bought one bottle of wine. We usually drink two or so, and one of our bottles of home brewed black cherry wine in the basement had popped its cork. So you know what that means… *Darn it, we had to drink the other bottles before they blew!*

So, this was our week of paleo groceries. Keep it simple and buy lots of meats and vegetables, some fruits and a few pantry staples.

# A Week of Grain-Free / Paleo Meals

I'll list our meals for the week, and a few details of how I worked out what to do with everything.

First of all, I took the cauliflower and made it into a big batch of cauliflower rice that I kept in the fridge. Cooking it up takes less than 10 minutes, once I have it chopped by the food processor. I also baked a whole winter squash in the oven, removed the seeds and skin, and pureed the flesh to use easily during the week.

**Sunday**

Breakfast: Pumpkin muffins and scrambled eggs

(Late breakfast, so we skipped lunch, as we often do on the weekends. Just had some homemade pastrami and apples as a snack.)

Dinner: Oxtail Braised with Red Wine, Orange & Rosemary, Root Vegetable Purée, homemade Sauerkraut and a green salad

**Monday**

Breakfast: Leftover pumpkin muffins, scrambled eggs

Lunch: Leftover Oxtail with extra greens and Cauliflower Rice

Dinner: Italian meatballs, tomato sauce, zucchini noodles– I made the noodles with a spiralizer for the first time– loved the results!

**Tuesday**

Breakfast: Grain-free Dutch Baby for Jeff and Amelia and I'll admit it– I had some fresh vegetable juice in the morning, followed by almonds and dark chocolate!

Lunch: Amelia had leftover meatballs with marinara dipping sauce, olives and cucumber slices. I had a big green salad with tuna, sunflower seeds, red peppers and tahini dressing.

Dinner: Moroccan Beef Stew with Cauliflower Rice and homemade Sauerkraut

**Wednesday**

Breakfast: Jeff and Amelia had eggs and fruit. I had grapefruit and avocado, drizzled with olive oil and sea salt. (I know it sounds weird, but I liked it!)

Lunch: Leftover Beef Stew, Amelia had leftover Chelo Kebab that I had frozen last week, plus cucumbers and fruit and a Tahini Molasses Cookie

Dinner: Roasted Chicken, roasted butternut squash, and warm leeks in vinaigrette, and homemade Sauerkraut

(After dinner, I shredded the leftover chicken to use in another meal, and put all of the bones plus one more from the freezer into the stock pot to make bone broth with.)

**Thursday**

Breakfast: Jeff and Amelia had buttered sweet potatoes, since we were out of eggs. I had fresh vegetable juice and then scrambled eggs after I went to pick some up.

Lunch: Jeff took the last of the beef stew, with winter squash puree; Amelia had leftover Chelo Kebab that I had frozen last week, plus cucumbers and fruit and a Tahini Molasses cookie. I had a somewhat random lunch of roasted chicken, a mug of beef bone broth, and homemade tahini crackers with butter.

Dinner: Mediterranean Chicken Soup with homemade veggie crackers (very experimental) and butter.

**Friday**

Breakfast: Eggs with sauteed onions sprinkled with thyme, and fruit

Lunch: Amelia and I had tuna salad and veggie crackers, Jeff took leftover chicken soup.

Dinner: Chelo Kebab and Cauliflower Rice, with olives, Tahini Sauce, cucumber slices and homemade Sauerkraut

**Saturday**

Breakfast: Shakshukah (without the cheese in the recipe, using zucchini and no eggplant)

Lunch: Tuna salad made with celery, olive oil, lemon juice green olives and chopped sun dried tomatoes. We ate this with carrot sticks and cucumber slices followed by apples.

Dinner: Chicken and vegetable soup

A couple other notes... We drink coffee every morning, and I did one big batch of juicing and froze individual portions for us during the week. (That explains the big bowl of carrots, and accounts for most of the celery and all of the beets.) Amelia takes a little jar in her lunch to school each day. Also, we usually have either bacon or breakfast sausages to alternate with eggs– this was an unusually monotonous week in that regard!

As I'm sure you have noticed, I am a huge fan of leftovers. You don't have to eat the same thing over and over again, though. Invest in a good set of glass storage containers, and cook more than you will need. Freeze or refrigerate individual portions to take for lunch later that week, or in the next week. We don't mind having one meal twice in a row or in a couple of days, so I usually make twice as much as we need– either for a whole supper soon after, or for lunches. This is such a win-win-win, as it saves time, money and mental energy.

And at the end of the week, we still have a few veggies left over, an avocado, a little more shredded chicken, chicken stock and some frozen kebab for Amelia's lunches sometime that week. So, we ate most of it, but never ran out of food– just right!

**I hope this list is helpful for you, and that making meals for the family from scratch looks just a little more do-able now.**

# Let's Talk About Food Attitudes

Before we part, I'd like to talk to you a little bit more about food attitudes.

I have been very guilty of approaching food with the wrong attitude, and am afraid I contributed to an orthorexic culture. (Orthorexia is the eating disorder in which people are obsessed with the health implications of the food they eat, leading to real fear of food.) Having this little talk and approaching food with a much-changed attitude is one of the ways in which I try to participate in healing this issue.

When I started cooking as an adult, I was vegan- for five years. I did that because I was really concerned about my health, and at the time, forgoing animal foods (and saturated fats) was the prevailing health trend. I did that. I did the vegan thing *meticulously*, adding anything I thought I needed through supplements, and trying to get as much nutrition as I possibly could, cooking everything from scratch, etc. I didn't eat junk food, fast food, or much sugar. Despite all of that, my health really suffered. I was becoming more and more ill, despite doing everything "right." Lots of different things happened that made me realize that I needed to start adding animal proteins. And the more I added, the better I felt.

As I continued adding more foods, I realized that I was experiencing more and more freedom to enjoy community and feed the people around me. I was also just enjoying life more.

The conviction has stayed with me, however, that the way we eat matters.

I am no longer vegetarian, and I genuinely love eating meat. I am a strong advocate for supporting ethical, sustainable food growers-- especially people who are producing meat responsibly and humanely. I feel strongly about this. If we don't support ethical meat producers, then they will go out of business and we will lose them. We will be stuck with the cruel and dirty industrial system for raising meat. Choosing to eat well and to support people who are doing things right is powerful, and can be such a source of joy when we sit down to eat.

We started eating a more paleo/ primal diet when we were in Germany, and it made a big difference for us, as well as solving some issues we had with food allergies and coordinating everyones' dietary needs-- my husband and daughter each had individual sets of food allergies. It made a huge difference for all of us, and we love eating this way. That doesn't mean that I think everyone should, though.

Here's the thing about food. Food is supposed to be a really joyful, stress-relieving element in our lives. The physiological process of eating is inherently calming and soothing-- it makes our nervous systems calm down. Eating is meant to be nourishing, on so many levels: our spirits, our souls, bringing community, a source of beauty and a sensual experience.

I'm concerned about a lot of the talk about food that goes on in "health" communities. It seems like there is a lot of joy lost over food. Lots of rules, legalism, fear and guilt. How tragic! It's not supposed to be that way!

If you find out that certain foods make you feel lousy, you should definitely eliminate them-- the goal being the restoration of joy to your mealtimes, not some intense regiment of eating rules. I would never tell you to just cut out a whole bunch of foods out of principal. We should eat what makes us feel great, and be able to sit down at the table and find nourishment, enjoyment and community.

Even though we've had a great experience with doing the grain-free thing, and have learned a lot about how different foods affect each of us, I wouldn't tell everyone to eat the way that we do.

Take the time and make the space to find out how different foods make you feel. (Elimination diets can be really helpful in this regard.)

Sit down, eat really great food, enjoy your food and the people you are at the table with. Food is a gift, and should be celebrated daily.

# Index

## About the Author

Ariana Mullins is an American writer, cook, explorer and photographer. She writes about her family's stories of challenge and adventure as expats in Europe, as well as inspiration for living a simple and meaningful life at AndHereWeAre.net. A passion for restoring lost kitchen arts and an adventurous spirit leads her to share her experiences in foraging, butchery, home brewing and anything new she can get her hands on in her (at the moment) English kitchen.

# Let's Keep in Touch!

I've loved sharing my table with you! You can find more recipes and follow along on my family's adventures on my blog And Here We Are... at AndHereWeAre.net. I'd love to have you sign up for free weekly updates, while you're there.

You can find me on social media, too!

• Facebook: https://facebook.com/pages/And-Here-We-Are/

• Instagram: http://instagram.com/andhereweare

• Pinterest: http://pinterest.com/andhereweare/

# Travel Photos

Here is a description of the photos you have seen in this book.

Country Path Along the River Orr, Suffolk, Page 23

Kitchen Garden at Wyken Vineyards, Suffolk, Page 42

Olives at the Saturday market in Brugges, Page 51

Cattle Grazing in Dedham Vale, England, Page 58

Grapes at Wyken Vineyards, England, Page 63 and 67

Coastal Mountains in Tenerife, Spain, Page 86

An Ewe and Her New Lamb at Wyken Vineyards, England, Page 103

Autumn Woods At Killarney National Park, Ireland, Page 105

Orford Castle in Suffolk, England, Page 108

A Bluff at the Coast in Orford, England, Page 109

Ancient Building in the middle of Brugges, Page 114

Enchanted Cottage in Norfolk, England, Page 115

Orange Groves in Kemer, Turkey, Page 128

Orford Castle, Suffolk, England, Page 129

Volcanic Beach in Tenerife, Spain, Page 132

Sunflowers at Wyken Hall, Suffolk, England, 143

A Walled Kitchen Garden at Wimpole Estate, Cambridgeshire, England, Page 150

Country Scene in Suffolk, England, Page 159

Made in the USA
Lexington, KY
22 December 2014